About the author

Christopher Ross is a Yukon-based print journalist and news photographer. Writing under the name Chris Beacom, he has covered life in northern Canada and Alaska for the *Dawson City Insider*, *Yukon News*, *The Globe and Mail* and *The New York Times* since 1994. He is also the author of *22: Christmas Without You.*

About the cover

A former Yukon government ferry worker stops to pose for the Dawson City Insider's *Know Your Neighbour* column photo in 1998. He quit in political protest, laying down his sign and vest. He has not been seen in the Yukon since.

THE UNRAVELING OF THE DAWSON
CITY INSIDER, 1997–99

Christopher Ross

THE UNRAVELING OF THE DAWSON CITY INSIDER, 1997–99

Vanguard Press

VANGUARD PAPERBACK

© Copyright 2021
Christopher Ross

A CIP catalogue record for this title is
available from the British Library.

ISBN 978 1 784658 72 4

Vanguard Press is an imprint of
Pegasus Elliot MacKenzie Publishers Ltd.
www.pegasuspublishers.com

First Published in 2021

Vanguard Press
Sheraton House Castle Park
Cambridge England

Printed & Bound in Great Britain

Dedication

For Emmett

Acknowledgements

I would like to thank Kim Marceau for her continuing dedication to this project, good journalism and an ongoing pursuit of justice and the truth, no matter how distant those concepts may be from what she sees and hears daily. Kim was the motivation for many of the stories we covered in the Insider and an inspiration behind the writing of this book. She was a brave journalist in the 1990s when faced with opposing forces ranging from hungry bears and unpredictable politicians to hunting down interviews at fifty below. She has a well-deserved voice in this story.

I would also like to thank Mike Rice of Catalyst Communications in Whitehorse, Yukon for his help at designing the covers.

Finally, I would like to thank the residents of Dawson City, Yukon, yesterday, today and tomorrow for continuing to create incredible stories that simply are not found anywhere else. May they always be shared.

Chapter 1
Toe Mile Hill

Yukoners know it as Two Mile Hill, but I will always think of it as Toe Mile Hill.

After twenty-five years in Canada's most northwest territory, the wince I make every time I go up and down that painful road has yet to fade.

It doesn't matter if I'm biking or driving, I hate Two Mile Hill.

This tale goes back to 1994, when I travelled forty hours by Greyhound bus from Calgary to Whitehorse for a possible job at a small-town newspaper in Dawson City, Yukon.

This brutal journey seemed to swallow people.

Riders simply disappeared off the bus into deserted landscapes surrounding Pink Mountain, Toad River and Muncho Lake.

Today, those people are ghostly memories because so many of the roadhouses that helped establish the Alaska Highway are now closed. No one gets off the bus anymore.

Times have changed.

The quickly formed relationships that were shaped by long hours resting on each other's shoulders in cramped bus seats were dissolved each time the driver yelled, "Rest break, ten minutes!"

We would all get up and trudge off the bus. Moments would end.

The Alaska Highway winds forever through the heart of Canada's energy sector before finishing in Fairbanks, Alaska.

It begins northwest of Edmonton in Dawson Creek, runs north through eastern British Columbia past several cities, then towns, then boarded up or barely alive roadhouses.

The highway then enters the Yukon Territory, skirting the pristine and wild Rocky Mountains to the south of the BC — Yukon border.

While riding the bus, I learned there is a direct correlation between geography, selection and prices in northern Canada: further north meant less selection which meant higher prices.

A five-dollar double decker cheeseburger in Edmonton turned into a ten-dollar grilled cheese sandwich in northern BC.

I had just finished my first year of the two-year Journalism Arts program at the Southern Alberta Institute of Technology (SAIT) in Calgary.

I certainly couldn't afford a ten-dollar grilled cheese sandwich.

Like many students, I was broke in pocket but not in spirit. Considering the price of a gas station goodie, heading north probably wasn't going to make me any wealthier.

However, finding a job in journalism was never going to be about money. I hoped it would simply lead me to interesting people and stories.

While planning our summer job hunt, my school friends and I made three simple rules.

These rules focused on finding a summer job in a fun and funky town, not some dismal road-to-riches resource centre bisected by a highway:

1. do not apply for a job east of Deerfoot Trail, the road that creates a border between Calgary's social classes by separating the thousands of kilometres of prairies that lie to the east with the beautiful Rocky Mountains to the west.

2. do not apply to a place name that begins with Fort (e.g. Fort Smith, Fort Good Hope, Fort Chipewyan, Fort Macleod, etc.). Too rustic. Too scary.

3. do not apply to a place name that begins with royalty. (e.g. Queen Charlotte Islands, Prince George, Prince Rupert). Too resource-driven, meaning a lot of alcohol-related petty crime — ultimately leading to a summer of ambulance chasing.

Heeding these rules, I was en route to Dawson City, Yukon, chasing my dream of working as a newspaper journalist in Canada's far north.

A school friend of mine had mentioned the Yukon as a potential for summer employment, as he had once worked as a surveyor near the Arctic Circle.

"Do you like dancing girls?" he asked me.

Of course.

"Do you like gold, wild bars and casinos?"

Hello! What's this place called?

"Dawson City," he said, promising, "it's nuts in the summer."

I had never heard of it.

But it met our three rules.

So, still in the stone age of pre-internet research, I went to the school library and pulled the bible of registered publications that were operating across Canada.

Sure enough, Dawson City had a newspaper — the *Klondike Sun*!

I found a phone number, rang up the office and received good news from the president of the society that ran the non-profit, independent monthly newspaper.

They did, in fact, have a summer student position and the job was opening up in a few weeks.

"Fax or mail us a resume," she said.

I did. I got a call back soon after. She said they'd love to interview me.

I asked her when an appropriate time was, and she said anytime. Just come on up.

Ha! There was a hitch. Isn't there always a hitch?

The interview could only be held in person. Others were applying. They wanted the job filled in early May.

School had been out for about a week.

"And if you come, bring a tent because there is nowhere to stay," she warned. "Also, bring a good pair of boots — it's muddy here."

Then she hung up.

I had a week to decide what to do.

And that was that. Either I travelled north forever for a sniff at the only job I could find, or I didn't.

It was all up to me — no handholding, no promises, only threats of homelessness encased in mud and a six dollar an hour job that didn't pay overtime. Daunting.

But there was nothing to hold me back, either.

What's a little mud? A few hours on the bus?

And I had a tent.

I looked at the map. I followed my finger west and north, west and north, then west again and still further north until it planted on a dot near the top of the map.

Holy cow! Where is this place?

Calgary in 1994 was not great for finding any work, much less junior work in a new field. My options were few.

Why not?

I dusted off my backpack and started to figure out how to get to the central Yukon as soon as possible.

A week later, the bus unceremoniously dumped me at the Greyhound station in downtown Whitehorse, still six hours south of my destination.

The same faded blue, white and red Second Avenue bus station, on the banks of the Yukon River, now sits deserted.

Greyhound no longer services Canada's north. This abandoned station was once the first stop for thousands of bleary-eyed, unaware travellers, landing in a new world.

It was May 2, 1994, and winter was still holding on in Whitehorse.

I got off the bus, stretched my crooked, cramped frame and looked north and south along the road, searching for proof that I was doing the right thing; that I had made the right decision to give up the small life I had in Calgary for a chance at a bright future in a career that I hoped I would love.

I didn't find that proof in front of the dilapidated bus station. Not even close.

I only found grey. This uninteresting stretch of blacktop could lie in any Canadian town — Prince This, Queen There, Fort Something.

I had bused two thousand six hundred kilometres and Whitehorse appeared no different from any other small Canadian city.

In fact, it looked worse.

What had I done? How did Whitehorse escape our beer-formulated rules for finding a super summer job?

I noticed a bleak mix of closed small businesses still hours away from opening, neglected chain stores and an underdeveloped waterfront.

I also saw piles of gravel and dog crap swept into the gutter left over from six months of snow clearing.

The weather was ugly, bleak and threatening snow. The cold sun was just rising over aptly named Grey Mountain. Leaves were still a month away.

I was only a day or two behind winter's disappearance.

The summer sleeping bag I had packed probably wasn't going to do that night, nor the next. Maybe not even the entire summer.

Worrisome.

The steely, north wind blew cold in my face and the world I knew was far away.

With almost no money, only a fleeting chance at a job, no chance of any accommodation, and still five hundred fifty kilometres from Dawson City, I needed something to cling to.

A familiar Tim Horton's sign a couple of blocks away was as close to an anchor as I could find.

I was twenty-five years old and did not drink coffee. Yukon would still teach me this wonderful pleasure.

Still, at least this well-known doughnut chain promised warmth, semi-cheap hot food and reprieve from the bus scene.

This wasn't the first time I'd found myself cold, tired, alone and hungry in a strange place.

I once chose this lifestyle — in 1992 — when I packed my bag after graduating from the University of Calgary and trudged west until I made it all the way around the world.

The dragon tattoo I had inked above my left ankle in China reminds me still that life is about attitude even if that means a few rough spots along the way.

So, fear wasn't a motivator to keep me moving that cold morning. I had travelled before. Hunger was. And the optimism of building a career out of my tent.

We all must start somewhere.

Isn't a sense of adventure and desire to explore the unknown what journalism is all about?

What's the point of writing about what I already knew?

I decided to keep moving north and not get caught up in the hell that was downtown Whitehorse.

I have learned, over the past twenty years, that I was far from the only person who thought of turning back south upon hitting the uninspiring streets of Whitehorse in the 1990s.

In fact, it's a theme for many newcomers.

"Shithole," is the most common description for Whitehorse that I've heard over the years.

"Whitehole" is a close second.

Today, Whitehorse is much nicer. A series of land deals among the powers that be over the last twenty years shook the ownership of Whitehorse's waterfront out of the hands of powerful White Pass — the company that founded the route to the Klondike beginning in 1897 — and into the hands of local governments.

The waterfront has now been transformed from a series of claptrap, renegade squatters' cabins into a beautiful walking trail rife with cultural and historic attractions, funky shops and upscale apartments.

It's a great place to live, rest or play.

Not so in 1994.

Before leaving the bus station, I asked about a one-way Greyhound ticket to Dawson.

"No Greyhound. Not enough business."

But I thought Greyhound went everywhere?

"Norline," I was told. "They go to Dawson."

This bus service is also long gone, replaced by a series of intrepid entrepreneurs who have ferried people and goods between Dawson and Whitehorse until they inevitably burn out.

A one-way ride to Dawson was eighty-five dollars. This price! In a time of minimum wages under five dollars an hour and sixty cents a litre fuel.

Absurd! I thought. Eighty-five dollars was half as much as the entire Calgary-Whitehorse route. I refused the ticket.

There's that correlation again: further north meant less selection which meant higher prices.

It was my turn to get stiffed by everyone who had come before me. It's the same everywhere. Yukon is no different.

There is even a name for people entering the territory, ripe for getting fleeced: cheechakos. Yukoners remain cheechakos until they survive an entire winter north of sixty, then they are rebranded as sourdoughs.

With zero ready cash and no idea if Whitehorse

even had a bank machine, I figured I would stay relatively hungry until I got to my destination.

I finished my meagre breakfast and looked at my well-used right thumb, wiggling it for worthiness a few times.

I knew this was my only ticket north to the Klondike.

I trudged down Second Avenue past the odour of grease wafting from the previous night's Kentucky Fried Chicken leftovers, now composting in the dumpster.

The largest ravens I had ever seen were picking at the remains.

The smell followed me until the road bumped into Fourth Avenue. So did a couple of stray dogs.

Good enough, I thought, dropping my pack just beyond the intersection.

Fourth Avenue leads to the highway and the highway leads north. No sense spending extra energy walking, I reasoned.

I stuck out the tiny cardboard sign I had scrawled together at Tim Horton's.

I figured it would surely entice some driver to pick me up.

It simply said, "Dawson City."

Yukoners are friendly, right? I wouldn't be there long.

I stood and waited in the early morning grey, shivering with cold, sleep deprivation and hunger, the temperature right around freezing, my small breakfast long metabolized.

A kind woman stopped — offering advice, but not a ride.

"No one is going to Dawson now. If you want a ride, you have to climb Two Mile Hill out to the highway."

No one? Really? And what hill? I thought. Where was I going?

She drove on, not giving me a chance to ask for a ride up the road nor ask any further questions.

I trudged north, believing her.

Rounding a bend to the west, that's when the ache in my foot started.

The road climbed sharply and twisted in an S shape, leaving downtown far below.

Oh dear, I thought. It really is two miles up the hill. It's not just a clever name.

A day before leaving home, I was in the weight room, socializing with friends and not paying attention.

When I removed a plate off the bench press bar, I accidently grabbed the inside weight, pushing the outside weight off the bar — and crashing onto my right foot. The forty-five pound weight fell three feet, breaking the bones in my little toe into tiny pieces.

The bus ride, though horribly long and arduous, was great for sitting still and resting my injury — I was thankful for that.

But just a few steps into the long walk up Two Mile

Hill to its intersection with the Alaska Highway, my right foot was screaming under the weight of my seemingly heavy backpack.

I slowly moved along in the mud, cars whizzing by twenty kilometres an hour over the posted speed limit.

It took me most of an hour to limp up the long hill to the highway.

I felt like a cheechako and definitely looked like one. There was no sympathy from the drivers, now heading to work.

When I got to the top, I had two choices — hitch back south to home and safety or turn north into the wind and an uncertain future.

I faced north.

We don't forget pain. It's one of our strengths, protecting us from making the same mistake twice.

So, I have never again attempted to hitchhike north by climbing to the top of Two Mile Hill.

I drive or bike now, always wheels under me on Yukon's long and lonely roads. I also quit lifting weights.

A ride eventually came along — they always do — and I was so very thankful to be moved up the road, on to the next step in my journey.

I was dumped just twenty kilometres north on the Klondike Highway, in the heart of the boreal forest, surrounded by bush and silence — not a car anywhere to be seen nor heard.

The woman was right — no one was going to

Dawson City on May 2, 1994.

Why was I?

Welcome to the Yukon, I shouted to the endless trees.

Nobody heard me, my voice lost forever in the icy, northern wind.

Chapter 2
Dawson City Arrival

It was ten thirty a.m., and I was standing on the edge of the Klondike Highway, still hundreds of kilometres south of my destination of Dawson City.

I had hitched in many countries and I almost always accept a ride — no matter how short.

It will lead me to the next ride, the next adventure, the next place that destiny says I am supposed to be. I was always positive.

This time, I was not so sure.

Getting dropped on the Klondike Highway fifteen minutes north of Whitehorse seemed reasonable.

Until I was there.

Few cars were on the road. Hours had slipped by and I saw less than five vehicles.

Highway? I thought. Where was I going?

I checked my wallet. Empty. Even if I did get a ride, I had no cash on hand for food and only about fifty dollars in my bank account. Another year of school had drained my funds. That fifty dollars had to last until I earned and received my first paycheck, at least three weeks away.

I stood waiting and waiting in the silence, broken only by the cold north wind whistling in the treetops.

Ever the optimist, this time I wondered if I had a chance at a ride.

Would the next car stop for some poor cheechako stuck in the forest?

I wouldn't, I thought, preparing myself for an exceedingly long, slow day.

I heard the car before I saw it.

The engine was revved way too high for its own good. The squeal of the overworked fan belt echoed towards me from the south.

The vehicle was a blur as it raced passed. Someone was in a rush to get somewhere.

The car skidded to a halt as soon as it could — one hundred metres down the road.

I heard the shoulder gravel spit away as the car reversed towards me.

I walked to the aging, beat up sedan. A middle-aged woman rolled down her window.

She was no Mario Andretti.

"I'm going up to Dawson for business," she said. "I can drop you anywhere along the way."

Dawson! Yes!

I threw my pack in the back seat and climbed in next to her.

The car heater was a blessing as my shivering had not stopped for hours.

She hit the gas like Hans Solo hits hyper drive, my head slamming into the back of the head rest.

My very slow day was speeding up.

I watched the needle: 110, 120, 140, 150, 160 - then I stopped looking.

I closed my eyes. It was too much of a change from the slow-moving bus and arduous walk up Two Mile Hill.

I felt her go faster, the seat pressing into my back.

After a few calming breaths, I opened my eyes and looked at the speedometer.

Needle buried. Speed unknown.

She cackled, knowingly.

"I've crashed before," she said. "Some old truck. Rolled it twice. Wrote it off."

What the hell? Should I get out? Is this normal? Do all Yukoners drive like this?

I weighed my options.

I couldn't bear going back out onto the cold, lonely road. Then again, what summer job is worth a life-threatening ride?

Only five hundred thirty kilometres to go.

I decided to settle in, let fate have its chance. And fell fast asleep.

I woke up when we were airborne.

She was laughing as the vehicle bounced off the road.

Yukon highway frost heaves are notorious. They rise in the spring when the freeze-thaw cycle is at its fullest.

The driver used these giant bumps in the road as ramps into the ether.

She read the frightened thoughts of a Yukon cheechako.

"Oh, it's always like this this time of year. Don't worry," she said.

"Are you hungry?" she added. "I'm stopping at Braeburn."

The pangs of hunger immediately displaced my fear of a useless death.

"Sure, but I'm broke," I said.

"Don't worry — this is Braeburn," she said. "I can share mine with you."

Braeburn Lodge is a well-known roadhouse that is one of the last remaining anywhere in the north.

The straightening of the Alaska highway and fuel-efficient engines have rendered most of these historic rest stops all but useless.

People now zoom passed derelict, boarded up lodges that were once the essence of northern travel survival.

Somehow, Braeburn continues to thrive. Steve, an old biker, still runs the place.

His success?

The world's most giant food.

The driver ordered a grilled cheese sandwich for about seven dollars.

I expected nothing but two slices of Wonder Bread grilled just enough to burn the lowest amount of fuel possible to bubble up a single piece of processed cheese.

That's what my two days north of sixty had taught me: further north meant less selection which meant higher prices.

This time, I was wrong. I learned right there the north was not to be judged so quickly.

Out came a sandwich bigger than the plate. Almost a foot across and three inches thick, this grilled cheese could feed a family, plus the pigs Steve kept outside.

It was the largest sandwich I had ever seen.

Stunned, I gladly accepted a third of my driver's lunch, my only food for the rest of the day.

She drove north. I relaxed even as the needle once again buried itself at the bottom of the speedometer and the car continued to bounce over the frost heaves.

I would arrive in Dawson City in no time or I would be dead, long lost over the unguarded edges of this narrow, empty two-lane road.

At least I wouldn't go down hungry.

I remember little more about this drive.

I know the driver spoke uninterrupted for the next three hours.

I listened to every word about Whitehorse, Dawson, her start-up sign business and how the government was killing the Yukon.

It was all going to change for her in Dawson City, she said, being the first in a long series of gold seekers and entrepreneurs I would meet that summer.

We arrived in mid-afternoon, completing the journey in just over four hours.

I have since made this trip hundreds of times and she still holds my record for fastest drive between Whitehorse and Dawson.

She dumped me at the edge of town and went off to her big meeting in a small place.

I don't know her name and I haven't seen her since. I hope her business prospered or at least she survived the journey back to Whitehorse. I will never know.

I thrust my pack over my shoulder and walked north to the centre of town, legs aching with stiffness.

If winter was whimpering to hold on in Whitehorse, it was still fingernails deep into Dawson.

The pavement ended when the blacktop hit the edge of town, replaced with half-frozen mud roads lined with piles of snow accumulated from the ploughs working the streets over a long winter.

I thought this odd. Isn't it usually the other way around? Don't gravel highways tend to run into well-managed, pristine paved city streets?

Not in the Klondike, evidently.

Dilapidated buildings set high off the ground on blocks were still boarded over on Front Street.

It gave the impression that the town was deserted since it emptied, post gold rush, in 1902.

The woman on the phone from the newspaper had said, "bring a tent — people camp here in the summer."

Summer? The temperature was hovering around freezing. The north wind was literally blowing out of the Arctic Circle a few kilometres away.

Giant sheets of pan ice and bergs were floating lazily north, down the Yukon River, towards the Bering Sea.

The river ice had just broken up the day before.

I pushed on, looking for the elusive campground.

I asked someone passing by where I could pitch my tent.

He pointed back over his shoulder, hardly breaking stride. "Turn right at Riverwest," he offered.

I thanked him, moving on.

One block, two. I saw the original Riverwest Coffee and Natural Foods advertised in a two-storey log building, now long since burned down.

No one was there.

I turned right and walked a short distance. I found a parking lot the size of a city block.

It was flat and empty, not a tree, bush nor picnic table anywhere. Any signs of nature were covered by piles of dirty snow and muddy parking spots, mostly designed to pack in the hundreds of recreational vehicles that would eventually find their way north later that year.

My dream of a beautiful camping spot in the warm, scenic forest was quickly shattered by this uninspired parking lot in the centre of town.

An aged, hand-painted sign on the wall of a deserted office indicated I was in the right place: "Gold Rush Campground. Closed."

No one was around. The only indication that this was a place of camping (and nature) was the hand painted numbers scrawled on the overturned dredge buckets that gave the location of individual campsites still buried in mud and snow.

What the hell? I muttered under my breath, not for the last time.

The space was completely uninhabitable. I thought I would die if I camped there.

Completely perplexed, I was at a loss.

I had no idea where to go, where to stay, or even what to do next. Years of travel to countries around the world and Dawson City in early May had me completely stumped.

I stood there, wondering, wanting, needing… something! A sign, a hint, an indication that there was life out there — and that I could find it.

I looked at the towering mountain that looms over Dawson City, scarred by an ancient landslide that helped form the swamp that serves as the town's footprint between the Klondike and Yukon Rivers.

It's called Moosehide Slide or just the slide.

And there it was. My sign.

Partway up the pile of rubble at the base of the slide, I could make out a single blue tent.

It was a dot of joy in the white that still covered the lower mountain.

Life. Eureka.

I headed for the tent, following the fifteen-minute walk up Front Street to the north end.

I never made it to that tent. To this day, I have no idea who — if anyone — lived there. It could have been left behind from the previous summer for all I knew.

From time to time, I still thank that tent for being there — a beacon that showed me the way.

Years later, my wife told me she knew this girl, who knew a guy, who once tried to winter in a tent across the river in West Dawson.

He would spend everyday drinking coffee and smoking cigarettes in the Downtown Hotel, getting out of the life-threatening cold and darkness that sunk daily into at least the minus twenties.

One day, he was gone. Word is that he had seen Jesus in the night at forty below and simply left — leaving his tent and belongings in the snow until it was discovered in the spring.

I followed Front Street until it met Father Judge's grave and the Catholic Church property on the edge of the Yukon River.

Here, I saw three tents lifted cleverly out of the melting snow by pieces of discarded wooden boardwalk the municipal government uses as sidewalk on its mud roads.

The tents were dry. They looked warm and safe, well out of the muck and snow. A communal fire was burning. The view of the icebergs floating by was perfect.

It was a dream spot.

A young woman greeted me kindly, not the least bit surprised by my appearance. She smiled.

"Can't camp here," she said. "It's full."

Dream shattered.

I looked past her tent at the long stretch of deserted roadbed along the riverbank that once served as Dawson's dump.

Back in the day, refuse was simply piled onto the winter river ice at the end of this road, then cleared promptly by nature and a bulldozer in the melting days of spring. Bedsprings still push their way out of the riverbank today.

Full?

There appeared to be plenty of space. Still... respect is respect.

I listened.

"There's boardwalk up the hill. Go there," she said. "And come back and join us by the fire when you're set up."

It was my introduction to the Klondike's miner mentality — the ground you have is yours until someone says otherwise, pays you dearly for it, or simply takes it over.

And that ground is to be protected at all costs until it's abandoned.

For now, this little spot along the riverbank was her home. And she was standing by it. Squatter's rights.

I trudged up the hill as directed, finding a perfect spot for an overhead view of the Yukon River flowing forever into the north on its long journey to Alaska.

I found my own piece of boardwalk and dragged it into place. I set up my tent and stretched out, watching the icebergs drift by.

Well, here I am, I thought. And started to shiver.

Chapter 3
The Klassic

The 1970s-era 'Klassic' mobile home at Harper and Third is now abandoned.

The decrepit, single-wide trailer sits among the weeds, its roof full of leaks, the metal twisting and aging, cars discarded on the side.

It's a true wreck. It should be towed.

The Klassic was the first home of the Dawson City Insider. Let's fast forward from 1994 to 1997, to when I arrived for another summer in Dawson, just a few days after the Klassic was purchased by my former partner, Zig.

Zig is a great guy.

He still operates the same publishing business today, though the Insider was long ago laid to rest and our days in the Klassic are now distant memories.

These memories are captured only by the big blue box of aging newspapers that sits at my feet while I write, feeding my memories and this story. The Insiders are in mint condition.

My memories will be retained as long as these papers are kept from disintegrating. I've held onto them for more than twenty years.

Zig now has a real office. He still owns a mobile home.

Zig believes in this story, and I will truly attempt to represent him as we all see him — the adventurous, kind, generous, unique, and zippy fellow that he is.

God bless, Zig. Let the advertising revenue ever flow in his favor.

I was returning to Dawson for my fourth summer.

I had been teaching English in Japan at a private all-girls high school in the winter of 1996-97 when Zig had first introduced me to his start-up publishing company.

He had mailed me a copy of the first weekly Dawson City Insider, dated April 11, 1997. It was an eight-page, photocopied booklet.

The focus was on Dawson City's weekly TV guide. Zig had purchased the rights to the listings and was selling advertising around town to fill the guide. He was then paying to have the guide mailed out to every post box in town.

The Insider was free. The business plan was to have advertising cover the cost of the production and mail out, serving as a profitable marketing tool for his fledgling publishing company.

It was a great idea. The booklet was full of advertising, including a two-page centre spread purchased outright by a local realtor, who filled it with great Klondike real estate opportunities.

It was the most amateurish publication I had ever seen.

The front page boasted a scan of an old post card. It was a picture of Dawson City from the waterfront, but it was almost unrecognizable. It was too pixelated and greyed out. Zig was still learning how to use his new scanner.

There were no stories in that first issue.

However, the simple, copious advertising had me intrigued. Follow the money. I knew I could work with this.

"I'm swamped," Zig said when I phoned him from across the Pacific in early April 1997. "Come help." I promised to be there in early May then we both hung up. No details were discussed.

I considered my options. Dawson City was very far away from Japan.

Let me rewind to my first days in the Yukon in early May 1994.

I nearly froze that first night. The temperature dropped well below freezing and I didn't have enough warm gear nor food in my belly to keep out the cold.

The next morning, I walked my frozen feet to the army surplus store on Front Street and spent some meagre remaining cash on an army blanket.

The wool blanket was twenty dollars.

My choice was to eat well then or survive the next night's sub-zero temperatures. It was only May, after all.

So cold. So very cold.

I opted for the blanket. It was an easy choice. There was no guarantee one meal would keep me warm through another night. It certainly wouldn't keep me warm beyond another night. The blanket would.

Some new friends on the riverbank were in no better shape. One friend had lost everything when the Greyhound/Norline bus combination lost his backpack.

He had nothing. Not even a tent. Others pitched in to help. I didn't.

I remember him making Kraft Dinner over the fire with river water. No milk, no butter, no salt.

He was a happy guy. "It's cheesier," he said, when I asked him how it went down.

That's optimism.

The sun warmed, people arrived, jobs opened up and the summer of 1994 passed into my mind's own infamy.

I was a reporter when August dust finally settled, passing the true Klondike seasoning of being banned from a drinking establishment, not for drunken disorderliness but for simply reporting the truth. A customer had died from a cocaine overdose in one of the rooms for rent. Others partying with him spilled me their story because they believed a bad batch of cocaine was going around. The story ran in the *Klondike Sun*. The establishment didn't take so kindly to the bad press. I relished it. There would be other bars, other stories.

I had won a part-time job at the *Klondike Sun*, sharing the position with a co-worker who travelled almost six thousand kilometres from Ottawa to Dawson City to vie for the same job. Work opportunities in journalism were few and far between in Canada in 1994.

Despite my effort to get to Dawson, it was a job I was lucky to have.

Caroline Murray had graduated that spring as a journalist from Carleton University, recognized as Canada's top journalism program in those years. It may still be.

My competition for the position was fierce. So goes this industry. Caroline ultimately won the full-time position after the interview process. The hiring board kept me on part-time after they fired the current editor. Caroline and I agreed to share all the hours, and both take on a second job to make up the missing hours. It was a rare job-sharing agreement. It was far better than trying to hitch hike home to Calgary.

That summer, we learned to share the newsroom duties, pushing each other to write better, dig deeper, edit each other's stories, develop and process film in the darkroom, create newspaper pages using a combination of early generation word processing, a waxing machine and cut and paste technology.

We stayed up late at night building advertisements, updating the subscription list and coordinating volunteer proofreaders. The workday was often sixteen hours long, with no overtime pay beyond our normal seven-hour shift. Someone had to get the paper completed. That was on us.

When the *Klondike Sun* came off the press, we would deliver the new edition around town ourselves. The pride in our work, though still relatively amateur, was immense.

The summer ended and I returned to school back in Calgary to complete my journalism school diploma. Caroline moved to the daily *Whitehorse Star* and then on to a fine career in Ottawa.

My career grew as I travelled and wrote for several years, living nomadically as I searched for work and stories. Dawson City was always an option; always a place where I could find a special story.

My mind was made up about a return to the Klondike as soon as I got off the phone with Zig in 1997.

I abandoned my three classes of teenage girls with a quick resignation to the boss, though their beautiful hand-written, sticker-encrusted letters arrived in my post box in the Yukon for almost a year. Bless them all.

I jumped onto a Nagoya-Vancouver-Whitehorse Air Canada flight in early May and within a few days found myself at nearly the same point on the Klondike Highway as I was in 1994.

This time, there was no bus and no grind up Two Mile Hill. I was already ahead, it seemed.

The sun was shining, my belly was full, and I knew exactly where I was going and why.

In fact, after six months in noisy Japan, I was happy for the empty, clean silence of the boreal forest.

I smiled and relaxed in the warm sun, barely standing to hitch a ride.

I was in no rush to get back to Dawson City.

The town would be there in a state that would probably surprise me, as it always does. I could be patient.

Even as I write this, I think about heading north to Dawson City for a visit, knowing full well I have no idea what will happen when I arrive. Experience isn't the only teacher in that town.

There is something special about being in a small outpost surrounded by thousands of kilometres of unfenced, undeveloped forest.

The remoteness makes us seem so much smaller than in the south.

With our egos swallowed by the bush, we can easily form new relationships with anyone who piques our curiosity.

It's a great place to talk to strangers and be a journalist. People are open.

I must have found a ride. I have no recollection. I arrived on Front Street drama free, as if this ultimate transient town didn't care if I was there or not.

The streets were busy with people. The buildings stood guard.

Hundreds of thousands of travellers have wandered in and out of the Klondike since the gold rush of 1898.

The antiquated, beat-up buildings no longer paid attention to who came or went.

Dawson City is a municipality that is officially called the Town of the City of Dawson, but simply goes by Dawson City or Dawson. I will use both names in this story interchangeably. It doesn't really matter. Just don't confuse it with Dawson Creek, BC, which is thousands of kilometres to the south at the start of the Alaska Highway. That mistake will surely get you lost.

Dawson City was the largest city north of Seattle and west of Winnipeg in 1898, at the peak of the Klondike gold rush, which attracted at least thirty thousand people to the area.

Today, it is a small, isolated village located in the very large boreal forest. Gold, government and tourism support a population of around two thousand people.

Whitehorse is the closest major community. There is no notable population to the north, east or west, except for the small villages of Fort McPherson, Old Crow and Inuvik, which sits near the edge of the Arctic Ocean. Dawson City is completely alone.

With my pack, tent and sleeping bag once again on my back, I found the address of the Klassic trailer and walked to the lively mobile home that would become my professional office for the next year.

Full ash trays greeted me, decorating the front deck.

Smells of lunch and dirty dishes wafted out of the back door of the busy Westmark hotel kitchen that still sits across the street.

Zig shared the back bedroom with his girlfriend at the time and rented out the other two bedrooms.

His cramped publishing office was stuffed in the middle.

Zig was not there when I arrived.

Instead, I was greeted by a guy staring into a computer screen who said very little other than telling me to sit and wait for Zig, who would be back eventually. I only remember his thick black glasses and closely cropped hair.

A large black dog was curled up under one of the desks, patiently watching me.

We didn't talk at all as I waited. I ignored the dog.

Zig eventually arrived. It was good to see him, a relief after my long journey across the Pacific.

I asked if I could have a shower, stinking badly after my trip.

"No showers," he said. "My roomies and I agreed that only people renting can shower here. Sorry."

This was standard in Dawson City those days. I understood.

Suffering from a summer housing shortage for decades, turf was valuable. No freeloaders allowed.

Still, it was a bit tough.

I asked him about work.

Zig barely remembered hiring me a month earlier and certainly hadn't organized a position, nor thought of some sort of wage.

But he was right about one thing: it was obvious he needed help.

The office was in shambles.

White paper was scattered and piled everywhere.

Decorated with white walls and white furniture, it looked like winter was still alive and well inside the Klassic.

I watched the office activity for a while. Frenetic. Unorganized. Confused, but with limitless opportunity.

It was a potential gold mine, that was obvious. Digital publishing was all the rage in 1997. So was offering internet service. So was offering photocopying.

The white cordless phone rang non-stop, lost in the sea of white paper blizzarding the tiny office.

Watching Zig leap and search for the ever-disappearing cordless telephone after it rang, I quietly put forward a suggestion: wrap some orange flagging tape around its antenna so it could be found amongst the piles of paper when it rings.

Zig scratched his bald head then dug a roll of flagging tape out of the shed. He liked the idea.

I asked if I could come back tomorrow. I needed to find a shower. I needed to once again find a place to pitch my tent.

It was a good start.

Teetering at the edge of my future, I also needed a day to think about what could possibly lay ahead if I made this jump into the publishing unknown.

True, I had little to cling to. That also meant I had little to lose.

The student loan guys were starting to track me down.

And I needed a place to sleep that night. I wasn't going anywhere.

I went to Minto Park and played hacky sack in the sunshine with some old friends from previous summers, meeting up as if time had never passed.

Later, I once again found a spot in the north end next to the Yukon River.

There was only one other tent pitched that day. No one was around to lay claim to the best spots along the bank.

It was occupied by CWIB, the Crazy Woman in Black, who used to frequent Dawson City every summer until even the women's shelter had enough of her.

I was not entirely confident it was a safe spot to pitch my tent. But as long as I could continue to hear her talking to herself, I knew I was okay.

Then I went out and got happily drunk with old friends, letting the next day happen as it may.

The Klondike had welcomed me back with a bear hug.

Chapter 4
The Photocopier

"It's broken. Call Lenart," someone said.

Zig and I and probably others stood over the recently leased photocopier wondering what to do.

Zig's ever-present roommate, Dom, took it all in.

Dom was always quick to provide a suggestion while watching Zig's publishing empire grow next to his rented bedroom in the Klassic. He was our biggest fan.

Our empire building also gave Dom something to think about while he smoked.

And Dom smoked a lot. We all did. That summer, about eight out of ten summer transients liked to light up.

It was hard to avoid second-hand smoke, especially in the bars and restaurants.

Dawson City was a smoker's world until the Yukon government rightly banned tobacco from indoor establishments in 2006.

Pouches of Drum tobacco for roll-your-own cigarettes were cheap and popular.

We went to the deck to smoke, thinking and chatting about what to do. A deadline loomed and the copier was dead.

Again.

Rolling up our cigarettes, we all agreed the Xerox deserved the repair.

Zig had purchased the contract for Dawson City's television listings when he started the business.

With it, he saw an opportunity to sell advertising around the weekly reruns of *Cheers*, *The Cosby Show* and early season baseball.

The photocopier was critical to the process.

Theoretically, it really wasn't that complicated.

With the arrival of the internet into one of the world's most hard-to-reach towns, Dawson City could now receive information from anywhere in the world in a few seconds.

It was a true first for this town, which had somehow survived and communicated with the Outside despite a hundred years of isolation.

Letters, messages and packages were delivered by dogsled, boat, truck, airplane, telephone and now the internet. Dawson City always communicated.

But this was 1997. The internet was changing everything.

We simply had to plug a phone line into the back of the new Apple Macintosh Power PC tower and connect to the internet through the dial-up modem software to connect to the outside world.

B*waa beep, beep shhhh, wah, bong, bong, bong, bong, bong, bong*, silence — the inexplicable sound of manually connecting a computer to the telephone-based internet in 1997.

Horrible.

In Dawson City, the dial-up connection issues were severe.

Connection attempts were always unpredictable.

Pesky ravens, fallen trees or road digging equipment consistently damaged telephone lines anywhere from Edmonton to the Klondike, interrupting the data transfer. Locally, too many users on the system at once would also prevent connection or transmission of information.

And download speed? We are talking bits per second (bps) back then, especially when half the town was online, clogging the system.

The internet ran at about a thousandth of the speed it runs today. Maybe less.

So, the plan of a quick download of the TV guide, purchased and transmitted out of New York City, well, it never seemed to work out that way.

Back then, standard home computers only had two megabytes of RAM.

Running multiple programs at once was a risk if not a rarity. Computers crashed all the time when the RAM was full. Work was constantly being lost.

Publishing companies have a lot of files. A lot.

These files filled the small hard drives quickly.

Sometimes, downloading a file from the internet and storing it on the computer was like trying to stuff a thick document into an already full filing cabinet.

Eventually, the drawer wouldn't close, no matter how many times we tried to slam it shut.

And we slammed those computers hard.

Several options presented themselves to fix this: get a bigger hard drive, delete the old files, or just keep jamming files onto the hard drive and save the problem for another day.

We usually chose the third option to save time, albeit in the short term. We could worry about the long term later.

But the main issue was the inconsistent connection.

It would simply be lost. Gone. Kaput. Start again.

The download of a file that takes a second or two today could take hours back then.

This was not a good thing when deadlines had to be met.

Downloading went on twenty-four hours a day. A second phone line was installed into the Klassic just for the internet and fax machine.

The other problem was our overwhelming and early success.

Business is always frenzied during May in the Klondike.

Each year, more than one hundred thousand visitors pass through Dawson City and businesspeople line up on top of each other for a piece of the financial pie those crowds bring in.

The money season lasts only ninety days before the rush of tourists turns back into a trickle.

Competitive advantage is critical in the fight for tourist dollars.

Advertising? Absolutely.

I was still learning about journalism and had little knowledge about being an editor.

I had studied a year of digital publishing programs at school — PageMaker and Quark Express, though "study" was a bit of a stretch.

Fully inspired by writing, I put minimum effort into page layout classes. Little did I know how important this skill would become over my twenty-five year career.

So, for the first two weeks of work, I simply sat in a chair and learned.

I watched Zig work the computer keys almost maniacally — designing ads on Multi-Ad Creator, placing them on the Adobe PageMaker Insider template, downloading files, filling holes with whatever idea we could come up with — daylight hours, commodity values, classified ads, digital photos of local legend Diamond Tooth Gertie sitting in a patron's lap — fully pixelized in all her glory.

Despite our early problems, the publication was working and growing fast.

It was all because of Zig. He had an idea, an excitement and a refusal to give up.

He was also the best at keyboard shortcuts that I had ever seen.

"Forget about using pull down menus or don't bother working," he said. This skill was a big deal to Zig. We simply couldn't afford wasting any time. He was bang on with that. I became a prince of Mac keyboard shortcuts, but Zig was the king.

He wanted to make the information move as fast as his brain could think — and that's fast. The faster the process, the more money we could make. That was his logic. Accuracy was a distant concern for Zig.

With zero education in journalism or publishing, Zig was old school mentality running with new school toys, with just the right amount of craziness to make it all work.

We used to challenge each other to learn new shortcuts, especially on PageMaker.

Did you know you can kern one letter half a space with the right combination of keys? We learned.

The Insider was being mail-dropped to hundreds of post boxes around town and people were picking it up for free at all the bars, restaurants and stores.

Ads were working. People talked gold prices with us.

Business owners were easily convinced the Insider was a cheaper vehicle to relay their message around town than trying to do it on their own. We were something.

Zig had unsolicited advertisers walking in the door, ready to write him a cheque.

One day, I decided to try my hand at selling an ad.

The world of advertising sales was foreign to me but selling was not.

I spent a few months successfully peddling *Calgary Herald* newspaper subscriptions door-to-door when I was fifteen.

The boss simply picked up kids and then dropped us off in Calgary's worst neighbourhoods after six p.m. If we showed up on a certain corner at a certain time, we earned the privilege to knock on strangers' doors after dark.

A friend of mine, who had already quit school, got me the job. The boss would hire anyone brave enough to try.

We would work the dark streets and shady apartment doorways for hours.

The boss got a cut for the work the kids did while he sat in his car and smoked.

I made five dollars for each newspaper start I sold. We got paid cash each night. It was a good gig, an easy sell. We just had to be brave.

The job was perfect for a naïve fifteen-year old; perfect for learning the dark, unseen side of the newspaper world. Perfect for learning how to cold call.

I never knew who was going to answer the door. Some guy once gave me a Sony Walkman. No one was ever mean.

So, I wasn't afraid of cold calling. I relished it. I still do. There's a thrill to it.

I must have had a knack for it, as well. It took me just a couple of hours to score a heavyweight advertiser and begin changing the written history of Dawson City.

The Westminster Hotel has been standing for one-hundred twenty years. Duncan Spriggs was the owner at the time and may still hold the mortgage. Spriggs is an eclectic English migrant who arrived in Dawson City in the early 1990s, giving up British society to mine for gold.

Today, Spriggs is probably found gardening at home or sailing his winters away in the Caribbean. He has retired comfortably in the Klondike.

Spriggs did mine for gold, but his true success came from purchasing the Westminster, affectionately known as The Pit.

His other smart decision, in 1997, was to hire a manager by the name of Joe Urie, who had spent several summers in Dawson City working mostly in the service industry.

Joe was well-known, though we had never met.

I entered The Pit and sat down at a table, waiting and waiting for him to show. I waited an hour or more beyond our scheduled meeting.

I almost gave up when he came in. He had forgotten all about me. TV guide advertising was not on his radar that day.

Joe was larger than life and full of energy. About thirty years old, you could feel his charisma. He wanted to draw people to The Pit like miners to the gold.

That bar was going to make a killing that summer and he was in charge.

Joe is still remembered by many in Dawson City today, though he moved away more than twenty years ago. He now owns and operates the Jasper Tour Company in Alberta, Canada. I recently saw him smack in the middle of a nationally televised commercial promoting tourism.

I showed him our tiny, crappy, photocopied black and white TV guide and gave him the pitch — forty dollars a week for a small ad, sixty-nine dollars a week for a quarter page.

Immediately, Joe asked how much for the whole summer. I was gobsmacked. My heart raced.

My first sale on my first try. I'd never sold an ad before and I was about to close a deal worth more than a thousand dollars.

I realized right then we had something special. I scratched my chin and hesitated. I knew what a good thing I had to offer.

"Same price," I said. "It's already a good price."

Joe agreed, most likely knowing that just one round of drinks could cover the cost of a weekly ad.

The Pit sold many rounds of drinks back then. It sold liquor seventeen hours a day. It still does.

I went back to the office rosy-cheeked, with a spring in my step.

I booked the Westminster for the whole summer, quarter page, I told Zig.

He jumped out of his chair grinning and rubbing his bald head with excitement. Nothing thrills Zig more than an ad sale.

And selling a summer spot to a relatively huge anchor advertiser was a home run.

It was time to get publishing. It was time to sell more ads.

The photocopier had other thoughts.

Technical issues were causing the copier to hiccup in defiance; a full-on rebuke of what we were demanding from it.

The Insider was printed double-sided on eleven-by-seventeen-inch paper, then folded in half and stuffed together to create a booklet.

Back then, the paper had to be flipped around to print double sided.

Auto flip, double-sided, paginated, booklet printing off a photocopier was still years away for small businesses.

The Xerox paper tray held about three hundred sheets, though we would always attempt to stuff in much more than that. Just like the computers.

It hurts as much today to do the math as it did back then.

Let's see. An eleven-by-seventeen-inch sheet of paper could hold four pages of Insider, so two sheets would hold eight pages.

To print eight hundred copies of an eight-page TV guide, we had to run one thousand six hundred sheets of paper through the photocopier. But that's one-sided. To get it double-sided, that's three thousand two hundred runs through the copier, uninterrupted.

Just thinking about it makes me want to return to the deck, think and smoke. I'm still not sure if my math is right. It doesn't really matter.

And yes, of course we would mess up.

Sometimes, the pages would be put in upside down, so pages one and eight would look fine but pages four and five, which would print on the reverse side, would copy upside down.

Instant garbage. Huck them in the dump or burn them in the woodstove and copy again.

Often, we would find a mistake in an ad. Dom was the best at this. He'd casually pick up a copy and find the smallest apostrophe error.

Full deadpan, cigarette engaged, he'd say, "*it's* for sale, not *its* for sale."

Ugh. Reprint.

Sometimes Zig would just make the change with a pen directly onto the document, then copy the changes.

He hated going back. He'd shake off the mistake with a laugh. Time was money. The Insider always played fast and loose with the rules when Zig was around.

After too many copies, a long white line would inexplicably photocopy onto every page, cutting through the fresh black ink on every ad it passed. Useless. Into the wood stove.

We would open the copier, shake the last drops out of the Xerox ink cartridge and try again.

Finding ink in Dawson was not an easy thing. It could take weeks to get copier cartridges shipped from somewhere in the south. We were careful to eke out every drop.

By the first week of June, the strain on the copier was starting to show.

Advertising design contracts were coming in on their own and customers wanted inexpensive copies of menus and posters.

The photocopier seemed to be running around the clock. The telephone rang endlessly. People were constantly stopping by the office to rent time on the internet to check their email. We were busy.

Desktop publishing was in its infancy and we had our hands on the equipment to succeed. It was great.

The Dawson City Insider grew to twelve pages, then to sixteen — which meant more than six thousand photocopies were needed to meet the demand each week.

That poor machine had become a printing press.

And that's when the Xerox said no more.

A wheel from within the bowels of the copier actually came through the photocopying process, still attached to a page.

It was about a centimetre in diameter, but somehow the wheel glued itself to a copy as it whirred through the gears and mechanisms deep in the machine.

We laughed for a long time on that one. We still do.

With his quick eye for detail, I think it was Dom that pointed it out.

"There's a wheel on that one," he simply said, taking a drag.

That can't be good, I thought. How do we fix this?

Lenart was the Xerox representative for the entire north and central Yukon. He refused to work on the photocopier if we continued to have dogs shedding their hair in the office.

Zig always shook him off. After all, he had a contract with Xerox for repair. He demanded service.

Lenart could only be reached by radio phone because he operates an organic farm on the far side of the Klondike River from the highway. He started this homestead with a teepee in the 1970s. He's still there today.

Lenart is nearly completely inaccessible when he chooses to be.

Service repair from across the Klondike River? There are no roads over there. Lenart normally had to canoe to his pickup truck to get to town when he chose to drive to town. Sometimes he would forego the drive and simply canoe down the Klondike River into Dawson for work.

Really.

We found him early one Sunday morning by radio phone and into town he paddled. He had decided not to take his truck. It was his day off. Our TV guide emergency was not his emergency. It took him hours to show up.

True to his word, he fixed the copier as he did for clients all over the Yukon, replacing that oh-so-important tiny wheel, which was very hard to replace in the Klondike in those years.

He also gave us a stern warning. "You can't keep this up," he said. "It's not meant to print so much. And no more dogs in the office. The hair gets in the copier."

That's when the idea struck me to call the *Yukon News*.

Let's find out how much it costs to print a thousand copies a week, sixteen pages on newsprint, I told Zig.

Dom dragged and nodded in agreement.

Chapter 5
The First Edition

People understand the importance of their office copiers. No piece of equipment has caused more joy and frustration in the business world than the corner copier. Nothing has revolutionized the modern office more.

Oh, how amazing is our ability to spread the written word by loading a tray, pressing the button and then calling the copier guy when the whole thing breaks down.

Our little photocopy TV guide was swollen beyond control.

As I said, by mid-June, the Insider had grown to sixteen pages. This required four eleven-by-seventeen-inch pieces of paper, run twice through the copier times one thousand copies each equals eight thousand pages run off the photocopier! Maybe. Who knows? We just kept filling the paper tray until the numbers added up.

Zig wanted to fill every mailbox plus have extras for tourists and transients roaming the town. The circulation was growing.

Lenart was constantly in our office tinkering with the Xerox.

Once the pages were printed, we also needed to manually fold each one in half and stuff them all together in the proper order. This took dozens of hours, split amongst as many people as we could find to help.

When the wheel literally fell off the machine, I said it's time for a change and Lenart confirmed this. He didn't want to keep canoeing to town on his Sundays so that we could meet a Monday deadline. We all saw that we couldn't keep going this way. We were victims of our own success.

Zig's little publishing company was already growing beyond our control — after less than two months of trying.

The advertising was coming in faster than it could be produced. The desktop publishing business was thriving. We were backed up with orders for posters, menus, and rack cards.

The tourist season was just ramping up in Dawson City and it was optimistic and busy. Business owners and managers were banking on a big summer as part of the Klondike's centennial anniversary celebrations of the gold rush. They needed their marketing materials, and we were the only company in town that could provide them.

Gold was a big deal in 1898, when more than one hundred thousand intrepids took a year-long trip via several routes out of Edmonton, Seattle and Skagway in search of Klondike wealth.

Just one percent of those seekers actually got rich. We hoped to be in that lucky one percent by mining a new kind of gold – digital publishing.

This was 1997. People were buying their personal computers and getting online quickly, but most had no idea how to design a menu or create a poster using their computer.

I didn't think too much about the desktop design part of the business. I was far more attracted to the Insider. Plus, I'm a lousy graphic artist. I don't know any writers that thrive at this valuable skill.

If the venerable *Klondike Sun* could publish on newsprint, I believed the Insider could, too. It was time for a newspaper war.

I envisioned the glory days of the gold rush, when up to four newspapers once ran in Dawson at the height of the frenzy, feeding the news to over thirty thousand folks who had successfully made their way to the Klondike from Outside.

My experience working at the *Klondike Sun* in 1994 gave me every reason to be confident.

That paper, the only game in town for several decades, had become fat on advertising and a little bit lazy in its coverage.

Press releases were run verbatim, stories were generally conflict-free, and many were missed. I could take this battle on.

Zig wasn't so sure. He liked the idea of a generic TV guide that simply made money from quickly designed ads and light-hearted content.

Few readers complain about daylight hours or classified ads.

But Zig also realized that those limited costs weren't so limited anymore. The photocopier was having a heart attack, the hard cost of paper and ink was substantial, and too much time was spent folding and stuffing, even with the help of a summer student or two. We were losing valuable time that we needed available to make more money.

We both understood that if we could publish the Insider weekly on newsprint, we had a shot at taking some of the *Klondike Sun's* lucrative ad dollars. That idea attracted Zig the most.

I helped the *Sun* jump from a once-a-month publication to bi-monthly in 1994. It had stayed that way and was doing fine, financially.

No one actively sold ads at the *Sun* in 1997. They had been the only game in town when it was established by Dan Davidson and the Klondike Literary Society in 1989. The ad dollars flowed in on their own and Dan kept writing. The paper grew wealthy thanks to a dedicated board, a great rent deal with the municipality, occasional staff and Dan.

We knew taking on the *Sun* was possible.

To do this, we would become Dawson City's first weekly newspaper since the *Dawson Daily News* shut down after a fifty-five year run in 1954. Its building still sits in Dawson City today, fully restored and managed by Parks Canada.

We could bill ourselves as Dawson City's first weekly in over forty years. It was a good advertising pitch.

Zig and I agreed to contact the *Yukon News* and enquire about the cost of printing and shipping one thousand newspapers to Dawson City from Whitehorse.

The *Yukon News* was once an independent newspaper that was owned by one family for more than thirty years.

Its considerable success was largely a result of owning a web printing press in Whitehorse. The *Yukon News* is now sadly owned by Black Press out of British Columbia. It could be printed anywhere, if at all.

By the time someone reads this story, the *Yukon News* may no longer exist. So are the times we live in today.

But back then, that newspaper was a thriving warrior. It had a full roster of reporters and the seventy-two page; twice weekly paper was filled with advertising revenue. It was a big deal. Politicians cringed when a *Yukon News* reporter contacted their offices.

Printing the Insider — potential new competition — was fine with the *Yukon News*.

"It keeps my press rolling and my guys working," said Steve Robertson, the former owner. "I'm happy to help."

I had worked for Steve before as a practicum student in 1995.

When I drove to Whitehorse from Calgary in early February of that year, my 1983 Honda Civic hatchback broke down about an hour from town, never to run again, at least not for me.

I had caught some loose snow and spun sideways off the Alaska Highway into the ditch. The car and I appeared fine.

But the engine was packed with snow. It sputtered, coughed and died.

I spent five hours working on it with help from various passersby. Wet spark plugs? Maybe. But it was too cold to let the engine dry out and I had to move. The cold was setting in and I was still far from Whitehorse.

I abandoned my little Civic before the wolves arrived with the setting of the sun and the arrival of minus thirty-five degrees Celsius.

I thumbed a very sad, defeated ride into Whitehorse that evening.

Steve put me up for three weeks at the High Country Inn.

In exchange, I would work for free as a student reporter at the *Yukon News*. I was appreciative for both the opportunity and the free accommodation.

At the end of the third week, I remember being twenty bucks short for my forty-hour bus trip back to Calgary, so I challenged the editor at the time, Peter Lesniak, to a few games of pool just hours before I was scheduled to jump on the Greyhound.

Peter liked to bet.

I won the twenty bucks off him on the last shot and had just enough money to buy a ticket home plus a little bit of food for that long voyage.

I don't know what would have happened to me if I hadn't made that double-or-nothing final shot.

I try not to think about it.

Always, just make the shot. Never think about missing.

The point? The *Yukon News* was owned and managed by terrific people and I felt strongly that they would find a way to print the Insider affordably and efficiently for us.

True enough, Steve quoted a dollar figure that was surprisingly low. This lower cost meant far less production work for us and higher profits than using our photocopier to publish.

The price was so reasonable that we could budget enough money to hire another worker to help with all parts of the publishing operation. This would, in theory, free up time for me to sell more advertising. More time meant more money. So simple.

It was a eureka moment.

But there were some major hiccups to overcome before we could make the big jump to a weekly newspaper.

First, the newspaper itself would not be folded in half like our little booklet-sized TV guide. Rather, the Insider would be printed in full-size tabloid format.

This meant that I would need twice as much content to fill the pages. This was a big deal. This was an enormous step.

I was confident that Dawson City had plenty of fodder to fill the blank space week after week, but we had nobody to do the work to actually fill it.

Even if the advertising was pouring in, we had to generate enough content to fill the white space between the ads. I needed help.

There was also another bigger, technical issue.

Those in the publishing field, pre-1997, understand that a web press needs to have original documents printed out and pasted onto boards that are the same size as the final newspaper. These boards are shot with a camera.

A film is then produced which is used to create plates. These plates go into the press and the image is transferred onto the running paper through the inking process.

To do this, the *Yukon News* required that we provide tabloid-sized printouts of each page, stuck to cardboard boards, and taped together in proper order.

We had to figure out how to print all the pages on a full tabloid printer — something that we didn't have; something we couldn't purchase anywhere in the Yukon. Tabloid printers were a rarity those days. We were stuck.

Zig ordered the printer, but it would be more than three weeks until it arrived from somewhere south, shipped into Dawson City by delivery truck.

So, we had to choose between stopping production of the Insider for three weeks, sticking with the photocopier, or finding a tabloid office printer somewhere else in the Yukon.

The *Klondike Sun* had a similar problem. They had learned to print their pages in booklet format, then cut and splice them together to place them on the tabloid-sized boards. It was a long painful process rife with potential error.

Another phone call to the *Yukon News* solved this problem.

"Sure, easy," Steve said when we called him up and asked if we could use his printer.

Of course, he had one.

"You just have to have the boards ready to go to the press here in Whitehorse by one p.m. — same as our deadline."

Again, this is years before both the internet and desktop publishing programs were powerful enough to transfer the files to Whitehorse. The files were much too big, and the internet was still much too small.

Timing was critical to our operation. We had the rights to the TV guide and planned to keep running it.

The Insider had become our gold mine; our reason to approach every business in town to help them with all their publishing needs.

But even the TV guide was tricky.

To remain relevant, we had to print seven days' worth of TV listings and be sure to come out on time the next week. It was useless to print a six-day guide.

So, we had to work closely with the *Yukon News* print schedule and provide a seamless transition from the Insider TV guide to the Insider newspaper to ensure both our advertising clients and our readers remained happy.

We kept Monday as our weekly distribution day.

In those early weeks, this meant we had to have the digital file put to bed on Thursday night so that it was at the *Yukon News* to be printed on Friday morning.

We would then get the paper back to town and distribute it on Monday. It wasn't ideal — but with no tabloid printer in the office, it was a start — and our customers would remain happy and loyal. We just had to come through. Just make the shot.

I was trained and experienced in print journalism, had now sold and built the odd advertisement, learned the digital camera, designed pages on PageMaker and even organized subscriptions and delivery.

But publishing and editing our own newspaper? This was a giant leap for me. It would be a giant leap for anyone.

I could feel the fatigue from working at least fourteen-hour days, seven days a week, for seven weeks already creeping in.

I could feel the results on my body, soul and mind.

I was still homeless and sleeping in my tent on the waterfront next to CWIB. I was eating very little; driven by spirit, caffeine and the odd roll-your-own cigarette.

Zig and I had negotiated a loose partnership during our first few weeks together.

He had no payroll set up. He barely knew what money was coming or going.

We needed more equipment, more ink, more paper, more clients, more staff — more everything, I decided to invest my time and work then for a wealthier future later. I believed in long-term success based on short-term pain. I had nowhere to spend money anyway.

I told Zig I'd work for simple survival money in exchange for future ownership in the business. We negotiated one hundred dollars a week. I was fine with that.

A person can only take selflessness so far. Zig was in control of the cash, but I was in control of the Insider.

I realized I could work for very little but not on my own. I could never do all the work myself. I was a relative newbie to Dawson and far from being known as a local. Few people knew me in town.

There was plenty to worry about. If I was going to work for next to nothing, I wasn't going to do it alone. Zig agreed. We almost always agreed. We still do.

I was a twenty-eight-year-old optimist. Zig was the same. He worried little.

When things got tough, when key decisions had to be discussed and made, we learned to travel beyond the smoking deck and go for a beer. The Pit was our boardroom.

One day, probably a week or so before our first newsprint issue was due out, I went to The Pit and ordered up a tasty draft.

I needed to figure out how to fill all sixteen of those pages, renew and replace last week's ads and get the whole thing to Whitehorse to print in time to meet our promised circulation date. It was no small task and time was very short.

That's when I met Kim Favreau, and everything changed.

I asked if I could sit next to her at an otherwise empty table. I'd seen her walking around town. She was young, attractive and hip. She seemed harmless.

Kim has helped put this story together, and her memory of this very chance meeting is far sharper than mine. Let's hear about that first meeting in her words - let me pass the talking stick to her.

***

It was my fourth summer in the Yukon — third in Dawson City — the beginning of another few months living in a tent under the midnight sun.

I got a job as a nanny for a three-year-old boy. The first half-hour of my shift each morning consisted of rousing his parents from their hangovers, both constantly late for work, then clearing up the empty beer cans and cigarette butts from the yard so my charge could play safely outside.

I wasn't loving this gig. The parents blamed their perpetual lateness on me. More than once, I witnessed the father threaten and rough up the teenagers who frequented the youth centre next door. This was hardly a dream job.

One evening after work, I settled myself into The Pit for a beer and thoughts of a better working life.

As a third-time summer transient to the town, I naively considered myself a local. I thought I knew Dawson.

I ordered a pint, planning to shoot some pool for an hour or so before meeting up with my ride back to my tent on the Klondike River, just outside of town.

Earlier that day, I had picked up a copy of the bi-monthly newspaper, the *Klondike Sun*.

The front page featured a press release on the nearly completed land claim settlement between the Tr'ondëk Hwëch'in First Nation, the Government of Canada, and the Yukon territorial government.

Essentially, the feds provided the land and money, the territory committed ongoing support, and the First Nation, well, they got back what they had lost — their land — and a bunch of cash for compensation.

This land claim was an historic agreement. The Tr'ondëk Hwëch'in had been displaced by the Klondike stampeders a century before. That influx of gold miners, entrepreneurs and adventurers had forced the local aboriginal population out of the Dawson townsite, where they had traditionally fished salmon each summer before moving on to other areas in their territory.

The land claim was negotiated over decades to fix this harm.

The press release was written carefully by these three parties and released to the public.

The *Klondike Sun* had chosen to print it verbatim. No one at that paper asked the powers-that-be any hard questions.

No journalist was doing their job.

A guy walked up to my table and asked if he could join me. I thought I had seen him around, but I didn't know who he was or what he did.

I don't think he knew who I was either. But I said sure, inviting him to sit with me. We both had large pints of draft. We were both in Dawson-style duress.

As we drank, I told him how annoyed I was about the press release on the front page of the *Sun*. Where was the story? The conflict? I lamented that the newspaper had simply reprinted the press release as received, and on the front page no less. This was hardly journalism. This was propaganda.

That was when Chris told me he was the editor of a new start-up newspaper in town — the Dawson City Insider.

He agreed and told me to go find the story. Just tell the people behind the release that I was writing for the new Dawson City Insider... would I?

I had always been a creative writer. I was also an aspiring poet and hosted open mics at one of the local restaurants.

I had, in fact, recently walked away with some cash for the top spot in a performance poetry competition in Victoria — just enough to cover the cost of a meal and a bottle of wine. I could say I was a paid writer.

But journalism? I didn't even know where to begin... but how could I not? Surely this was not a chance meeting. Whatever it was, it was certainly a chance.

"Come to the trailer by five p.m. tomorrow with the story," Chris said.

I immediately panicked. How the hell could I pull this off? I had to take care of the kid the next day until then. I think I negotiated an extra half an hour.

I set out in search of the story behind the press release the next morning, three-year-old in tow.

This was 1997; there was no Google, so I ran around town, visiting the library, territorial government officials, the Tr'ondëk Hwëch'in leaders, the mining recorder's office.

I wanted to know what land the Tr'ondëk Hwëch'in wanted, compared to what they were actually getting from the government.

I imagined late-night, back room negotiations; maps upon maps pinned to the walls; secret communiques in the war room; hard bargaining — offer and counter offer of the land in question.

I may have been right, but I got nothing. Nobody said a word to me.

"But what land did you ask for?" I enquired at the band office — where I was quickly chastised for calling it "the band office".

I was offered no other information than what was in the press release. It was the same story everywhere I went — no story.

I was utterly dejected at my complete failure in finding the scoop.

At five-thirty p.m., I trudged over to the Klassic trailer, tail between my legs, embarrassed to admit my failure to Chris.

Humiliated, I explained to him what I tried to find out, who I talked to and how I couldn't get the story behind the press release. I was sorry.

Chris smiled. "Good. You've learned your first lesson. Want a job?"

***

When Kim and I discussed this project, I could only remember her simply working with me one day.

I had no recollection of how we met or how I actually convinced her to try to be a journalist with no training. I had no recollection of this encounter at all.

But when she reminded me of our first meeting, the memories came flooding back. They are kind.

How many people would take on a press release while babysitting and voluntarily start banging on doors looking for answers?

Very few. I was impressed.

I learned early on in school that newspaper reporting is not for everyone.

Many students headed for the exit door after the first week, terrified of making a cold call. Others drooled at the thought of barking at officials over the phone.

Nuts and bolts of writing and photography can be learned, but that fire-in-the-belly need to answer, 'what the-hell?' that's not learned — that's inherent and can't be taught.

It has nothing to do with a writing ability.

Kim had that. It was instantly obvious. That story in the *Klondike Sun*? She needed to know more and was willing to work for it.

Now, if I could just be the guy I told her I was — editor of the new paper in town.

Technically, I was up to speed. I knew the Yukon and where to mine for information. The business case for the Insider was solid and we had the means to produce and publish. I could teach Kim how to write a lead.

But to be an editor, I needed something to edit.

That meant I needed writers who wanted to write. Preferably for nothing.

We had sold twenty-five ads for the first edition of the Dawson City Insider newspaper, which was something — but not nearly enough to pay wages for several untrained writers.

This problem was overcome at one of our sit-down meetings.

There were plenty of drinking holes in town and they were all competing for tourists and thirsty locals.

Zig had spent three winters in Dawson by this time, so he knew more people better than me. He was accustomed to the barter trade and recommended doing just that to attract writers.

I agreed. I approached the manager of the Triple J hotel. I offered him weekly advertising in the Insider in exchange for a bar tab each week.

Through word of mouth, I attracted six writers to fill our first edition. Aaah, the power of free beer and food to hungry and transient tent dwellers.

For that first edition, Kim attended a school council meeting and learned there would be ten teachers leaving town and nine new ones arriving.

Allison Peake learned that the town's recycling centre needed to be better financed by government if it were to continue operating.

I learned that a producer for the Discovery Channel was in town shooting a documentary on Dawson City which would air nationally.

Darcy Kopas wrote what everybody knew — the rain wouldn't stop falling and chided that the streets were paved in mud not in gold.

Cecilia Greyson taught everyone that the powerful Dawson City Music Festival had finally found a permanent home, a year after losing its previous space (and all their records) in a horrendous fire.

Chris Dorey reported on what was new in town in his gossip column and we even had an advice columnist — our soon to be famous *Bartender*.

We intertwined these stories with the usual TV listings, CBC Radio schedule, a hand-drawn kids page by cartoonist Adam Larson, a youth photo essay courtesy of Shane Kurki, information about the upcoming annual gold panning championships, classified ads, a crossword puzzle, an editorial and an invitation for letters to the editor.

We also had all those committed advertisements. The Insider template was full. The paper would make a profit. For a first edition, I was pretty darn proud.

There was only one problem. By Tuesday afternoon, we still had no story worthy of front-page status. No deaths. No destruction. No crime. No mayhem. I had found nothing to attract the casual reader through a dramatic page one headline. How could we be the new paper in town if we had no real news? We couldn't just run some crappy government press release on the front page. Kim would walk away after just one issue. I was worried.

Then, fate being what it is, I suddenly found our story. Or it found us.

Someone burst into the office just as we heard the sirens. "Did you see the fire? Arctic Drugs is burning down!"

Arctic Drugs was located on Front Street near the General Store. It's no longer there. The fire took care of that. It's just an empty lot now, like so many other empty spaces in town.

Since the 1970s, hundreds of historic buildings have disappeared in Dawson City either from fire, abandonment, neglect or age because of the harsh next-to-the-Artic Circle conditions they must withstand, including hot summer sun, cold winter wind and wood-chewing flying beetles.

Without human support, the wooden buildings inevitably crumble.

Arctic Drugs had the look of a building that wanted out. Inside, stock was at a bare minimum and the owner looked to be the age of the near century old, one storey building. No one ever shopped there.

So, when I heard it was Arctic Drugs going down, I wasn't surprised.

We dashed to the fire. The whole town dashed to the fire.

Kim grabbed a notebook, and I snatched the funky new Olympus digital camera off the desk, all four batteries fully charged, providing enough memory and power for six highly pixelated pictures.

I can't overstate the importance of this camera to the operation.

I had spent much of my 1994 summer in the darkroom at the *Klondike Sun*, developing film, enlarging photos, cropping, cutting, pasting, scratching my head, reprinting my mistakes, inhaling toxic chemicals.

The process was painstakingly long, environmentally harmful and prone to error.

What a change in three years! For the first time in the history of publishing, we could shoot, view, delete and shoot again.

We could download, choose, edit, save, drop into the template, crop, and move on, all without any printouts at all. It all could theoretically happen in a matter of a few minutes.

No film, no equipment, no chemicals, no enlarger, no unventilated stuffy darkroom were required. Empty darkrooms now serve as legal marijuana grow ops all over Canada. Enlargers are in the dump.

Of all things that allowed two guys to create a weekly newspaper, our digital camera was the key. Just make sure the batteries were charged.

But I can't say the camera took good pictures. There was no zoom or depth of field, and resolution was minimal.

Kim talked to the police and the former owner during the fire. I tried to interview the fire chief. No one was talking. No comment was made about the cause of the Arctic Drugs fire that day nor any day.

I continue to retain my suspicions. So does Kim.

We ran the bare facts and a big picture in that gaping front page hole. There wasn't much of a story to go with the terrible photos.

We laughed when we saw the first cover of that newspaper. The firefighters looked square; their outfits were all corners, like something out of the Lego Movie.

Chapter 6
Midnight Run to Whitehorse

Around midnight, Zig, Kim and I finally filled in every hole to complete our first sixteen-page edition. The paper was put to bed.

This seems small, I know, but upon looking back through these pages, I can quantify the workload.

Let me do a count. That edition had thirteen stories, sixteen photographs, twenty-five advertisements, nine public listings, twenty-one classified ads, eleven separate TV listings and a whole lot of clip art.

Each of these items had to be contemplated, created, checked for accuracy, edited, cleared with a source or advertiser, fit into its own space carefully amongst all the other items and displayed professionally — no one wanted to publish a joke.

The word count was well into the ten thousands.

Finishing so close to deadline meant I had only hours to transfer the paper from the computer onto a zip disk and drive the paper to Whitehorse, six hours away.

The idea of flying to Whitehorse was not an option. But if there was a flight to catch in the morning, it would be far too expensive and would eat up any profits we would make on the first issue. I had to have the paper ready to print by one p.m. Zig and I believed glitches would be inevitable, and we couldn't rely on the *Yukon News* staff to fix any technical problems with our digital template. Someone had to be there. The Insider was my baby. It was up to me to go.

There was no way I could sleep that night and meet the printing deadline. It was going to be another long day. It had already been a long day.

So, with the hope that all the files and their accompanying fonts had made the technological leap from the desktop computer onto the zip disc, I jumped into the office truck — a rusted out but mostly trustworthy Mazda B2200 — and drove south into the midnight sun.

A late-night dusk was falling over the land. The Klondike highway was deserted.

I arrived in Whitehorse early in the morning and found space amongst the production staff at the *Yukon News* shortly after the office opened at eight a.m.

I had plenty of time to print out the pages on the fancy tabloid printer, run them through the wax machine and paste them onto the printing boards.

This should take an hour, tops, and then I would have time for coffee and rest; the first issue of the Dawson City Insider newspaper out of my hands and safe at the printing press. So, I thought.

I did receive some odd looks and glares as I fought for elbow room on the layout table that morning.

But, as I had recently worked for the *Yukon News* as a student, my face was familiar, and no one said anything.

I hooked up the zip drive from our office onto one of the *Yukon News'* Apple PC desktop computers and was able to read the Adobe PageMaker file.

The error messages started popping up immediately.

The idea of opening a simple PDF file was still years from being invented.

'Missing screen font' the computer told me over and over, as it attempted to read every file associated with the layout.

The computer had failed in its search for the fonts we had used in our layout back in Dawson that were not installed on the *Yukon News'* computer.

It's okay, I thought. I didn't care about the screen fonts, what I needed were the print fonts.

Back in the mid-1990s, there were two types of files associated with each font — screen fonts and print fonts. We needed both for WYSIWYG.... Anybody remember that acronym? What You See Is What You Get.

If both sets of fonts were not installed on the machine, then the computer would automatically choose a default font, destroying the design of the advertisement or text in question.

Courier was standard and might still be today.

It looks horrible. Nothing could look worse. Nothing was more worrisome than seeing Courier suddenly pop up in an ad that had been carefully designed, produced and signed off by the advertiser.

It was bad news.

I printed the pages and fortunately most of the advertising files were fine thanks to the beauty of the EPS, an Encapsulated PostScript file that is similar to an early version of today's PDF file.

Basically, an advertisement is created in a design program and, when saved as an EPS, the computer takes a picture of the whole thing and saves it as an uneditable version of the original.

This effectively captures all the fonts, clip art and photos that may be associated with the file.

So, I was in pretty good shape, but not perfect. I don't know why, but some of the ads still didn't print correctly; probably they were created directly on the page and not all the associated files and fonts made it onto the zip disc.

These ads were not in EPS format and print fonts were missing. Zig may have had a role in that. He worked very fast; details were sometimes missed.

I was stuck. An approved ad could not be tampered with at this point.

I felt the sweat bead on my forehead and my heart pound as I tried to figure out what to do. So far from our office, maybe five hours to spare until the press rolled, how was I going to fix this?

Where was I going to find several print fonts that I could run on a computer that wasn't mine?

I couldn't run an ad in ugly Courier and I certainly didn't want to leave giant holes in the paper.

I called Zig back at the office. He came up with a remarkable solution.

"I'll fly them down on Air North," he said.

Yes. Zig simply printed off the missing advertisements and put them in an envelope.

He then drove fifteen minutes out to Dawson's tiny airport and got the envelope on board the Air North flight to Whitehorse just before take-off. There was, indeed, a morning flight south that day.

Three hours later, I picked the ads up at the arrival desk in Whitehorse with an hour to spare before the press was scheduled to role — perfect.

I drove back to the *Yukon News*, careful not to spill coffee or get dog hair on the well-travelled ads.

I could now print out all the pages, wax them up and place them on their boards ready to print. I simply cut out and pasted the missing ads into their respective holes on the printed pages.

I did this ever so carefully, of course, as there was no chance at a reprint.

Thinking back now, I probably should have photocopied those precious ads in case I ruined them during the process. Hindsight.

My hand was steady, far steadier than today — no problem as I carefully cut out the ads with an Exacto knife. Everything fit perfectly in place. I breathed a giant sigh of relief when all the pieces were finally in place.

I then helped tape the boards together in the proper order. 1–16, 15–2, 3–14, 13–4, 5–12, 11–6, 7–10, 9–8. Is that right? I think so.

The first issue of the Dawson City Insider was ready for print, finally, and on time. Always be on time. Always make the shot.

The adrenalin drained away.

I felt like weeks had passed without sleep or proper food. Surviving on coffee, tobacco, stress and laughter, I felt it all start to crash down on me. I hadn't slept in twenty-eight hours at least.

No rest, I said to myself. It's summer in Dawson — the sun is high, and I have a new issue to create and just a week to get it done. There is no time for sleep; let's get going.

Two hours later, back in the truck and ready for another six-hour drive north, I had one thousand beautiful black-and-white newspapers ready to be handed out all over Dawson City.

I couldn't wait to start the process again.

I have since created over two hundred publications. I shine with the thought of completing each one. They are all my babies. That thrill of concept-to-publication remains in me. That's why I'm writing this book. I simply can't wait until it's done so I can start something else. I need to finish, then start again.

Since the first time I saw my by-line in a little-known soccer newsletter in 1993, until today, when I've somehow managed to spread stories and photos around the world, I've never been prouder as I felt in that moment when the first Insider came off the printing press.

We had made a real newspaper out of nothing but an idea and an over-worked photocopier. Dawson City had its first weekly newspaper in over forty years. It was time for a second edition.

Chapter 7
Ask the Bartender

Katie Grigor was born to be a bartender.

I don't know when I first met her. It was probably in the bar. That would make sense. I don't know when I last spoke to her. I don't know when she first came to Dawson City and I'm not sure what she's done since 1999.

I do know that she was my favorite bartender in Dawson for several years.

She worked at Peter Jenkins' Eldorado Hotel for a spell. She also poured drinks at four other establishments. The Eldorado was her least favorite place to work.

Peter Jenkins is the former long-time mayor of Dawson City and health minister for the Yukon government. He was a political behemoth in the Klondike for decades until he retired in 2012.

Hotel owners were the Yukon's power brokers for about a century, as the territory's liquor act did not permit the sale of alcohol outside of government stores, with the exception of hotels and restaurants. No bars were permitted unless hotel rooms were part of the establishment. To be considered a hotel, lodging had to offer a minimum of ten rooms in Dawson City and thirty rooms in Whitehorse. That meant Yukon's few hotels controlled much of the liquor trade, and with it the cash and power.

It was common for hotel owners to control local politics until about 2009, when the Yukon liquor act was changed to allow other establishments, like private stores and bars, to sell alcohol.

Up until then, any major changes to Yukon's legislative or policy framework was swayed by the hotel owners, and Peter just happened to be mayor, then the Klondike representative in the ruling conservative Yukon government. He may have been the most powerful person in the territory for the years that I covered him.

To dig out the roots of a good story in the Yukon, the hotels were usually a great place to start.

When I first went to Peter's office in 1994, deep in the bowels of his hotel, I expected to interview an affable mayor happy to spout smooth words to the press about his unique little town.

This was not the case.

Peter greeted me with a cold, icy stare. I quickly learned that he hated the press. I left that first interview speechless and a little bit frightened.

I thought I would be welcomed with open arms and a warm grin. I received the opposite.

Like all members of the press, he disliked me the moment I sat down. This meeting began a quiet battle between us that lasted the next twelve years, completed by Peter's defeat in territorial politics and the dismantling of his long-time dream of a bridge over the Yukon River.

But I'm getting way ahead of myself.

After that interview, I could only think about what he was hiding in his role as mayor.

I learned over the years that 'hiding' wasn't the right word. If people asked Peter for a straight answer, he provided it. He wasn't a liar. He wasn't dishonest.

People just didn't ask. Very few questioned Peter. He was fierce.

But I did. Often. And Peter always gave me answers, though the Insider was never allowed in the Eldorado Hotel.

Peter was a great mayor. Most of his decisions were populist and middle ground. He simply despised any opposition and he had little time for his council.

He knew what he wanted for the town and his followers continued to elect him for his strength and resolve. He was either loved or reviled. Consultation was not his strength. He said his door was always open, but nobody ever chose to go through it. Peter was the best thing that could happen to an aspiring young journalist, as long as I was brave.

Peter's greatest accomplishment was overseeing the crisis cycle when Dawson City floated away one day in 1979, thanks to a major flood.

The Yukon River flooded that spring after the ice broke and jammed down river from town.

There was nothing to hold the water back from emptying into town over the low riverbank.

In a matter of a couple of hours, many residents realized that their homes were sitting on a swamp at the confluence of two enormous rivers, not on stable ground.

Dawson's structures are built on blocks to lift them above ground and the murky, melting, moving and muddy permafrost.

There are very few basements. There is no concrete anywhere in the Klondike.

The ground has been thawing since 1897 when the town's fathers believed this swamp to be the best place to set up a series of docks and warehouses necessary to transport goods and gold in and out of the area.

Shadowed by a sun-blocking mountain most of the year, Dawson City was a terrible place for humanity. It still is.

The new residents quickly stripped all vegetation and put in lots and roads as quick as they could in 1898, the year of the massive Klondike gold rush.

Manmade infrastructure replaced the berry patches, spruce and birch trees that kept the soil together in a semi-frozen state. When the vegetation was removed, the town began to sink.

It's still sinking. The ground is always shifting. Roads and sewers are in a constant state of repair.

With no foundations to hold them in place, many of the houses simply floated away during the 1979 flood.

Some were found downriver; others were found across town.

The place was a mess, but it survived. Peter ensured this and the town didn't forget. He remained mayor off-and-on for more than two decades.

Peter brought in the army, literally and sole-sourced out gravel supply contracts to his friends. The gravel was used to build a mile-long dyke that still protects the town from the rushing waters of spring. The army did the work to build the dyke.

The town has not flooded since. Peter accomplished a great thing.

The other great thing he did was to oversee the hiring of Katie to manage his bar, the Sluice Box Lounge. No one called it that. Everyone just called it The Eldo.

The Eldo attracted the mining, trucking and big engine crowd. People who went to The Eldo didn't go to the other bars. They were loyal to Peter and stayed there.

I wasn't one of those guys.

I went to The Eldo because I liked Katie. She always made me laugh.

Katie was tall, lean, social and smart. She paid attention to everything. She understood her clients well. Nothing got past her.

I would stop at The Eldo when I knew Katie was working, usually in the late afternoons.

She was always a welcome respite from whatever mayhem I was involved in or chasing down.

She would help me to either forget my troubles for an hour or give me advice on what to do. She always made time to talk. She loved being a bartender.

We both did our best to avoid Peter Jenkins.

I stopped in for a beer at The Eldo one afternoon when we first decided to jump to newsprint.

I was thirsty and needed a break from the photocopier's never-ending clanking. I also had to figure out how to get content to fill the new paper.

That's when the idea struck us both for Katie to write an advice column in the new Insider.

I might as well have handed her the keys to the city.

She lit up. We were going to make her a star. Katie jumped at the opportunity.

Katie's *Ask the Bartender* advice column was born there and then.

No other piece of journalism, no matter how insightful, newsworthy or entertaining attracted readers to the Insider like *Ask the Bartender*. It was a hit from the first edition.

Each week, I would dutifully wander around town delivering free copies of the Insider to tourist traps and nefarious watering holes.

I would see an unwashed, unshaven gold miner turn straight to the back pages of the Insider, taking in Katie's advice over a cold draft and a lengthy cigarette.

That miner, often having spent weeks in the woods, simply wanted to read how a seventeen-year-old girl should best get over being dumped. Or where to find the best deals in Dawson when someone had no money. Even miners like mindless gossip.

It was amazing.

Long before most of us had an email address, advice questions would simply land on our steps at the Klassic.

I would pass them over to Katie at the bar. Each week, she'd answer the questions, and I'd pick up the handwritten responses during her next shift. She never missed a week until she missed all of them. It was a great time, and we had a great time. There were a ton of giggles.

Katie lives in Victoria now. She probably still gives advice to somebody, somewhere, all the time.

She's forever a bartender at heart and sometimes a writer. I caught up with her after twenty years. She was easy to find. I had plenty of questions for her.

***

Q: It's nice to find you again. It looks like you wrote sixty-six columns of *Ask The Bartender*. Is this number significant to you?

A: I have no idea how many I wrote honestly, but that sounds about right to me. Is sixty-six a significant number to me?

Well, it wasn't until just now, but let's see… sixty-six is the year that *Star Trek* first aired on TV; the year that mini-skirts hit mid-thigh (I've always loved my mini-skirts); the year Pampers created the first disposable diaper; and the year that James Brown first appeared on *Ed Sullivan*.

Sixty-six was also the year that thousands of fans burned their Beatles albums in response to John Lennon's comment that the Beatles were bigger than Jesus and David Bowie released his first single, *Can't Help Thinking About Me*. So yes, sixty-six… definitely significant.

Q: That adds up to about three hundred questions for a town of under two thousand back then. Are you surprised?

A: Holy cow. So, what percentage of year-round Dawson residents would that have been? Three hundred questions is nothing to shake a stick at, is it?

Q: How did you come up with *Ask the Bartender*?

A: I was tending bar in the daytime at the Eldorado Hotel and when it was slow, I'd have a lot of the kitchen staff and their friends come in after their shifts and sit at the bar and gab. They'd tell me their problems and I'd jokingly tell them what to do, whether they liked it or not.

I think you may have sat in on one or two of those sessions and I told you that if you were going to start a paper, you should give me my own advice column.

I was such a shy, demure thing back then, wasn't I?

Q: As I go through the old papers, the sub headline changed from 'Get your life in order' to 'Set your life straight,' so which one is it?

A: I think it was set your life straight... not sure who came up with that, but it wasn't me. These days I crave more order, so I'd probably aim for the first one.

Q: What does bartending have to do with advice?

A: Dude, everyone knows that when you're feeling down and want to toss back a few and pour your heart out, the bartender is your best friend and a captive audience.

There's an old saying that goes, 'Sometimes you meet someone that makes your life better — these people are called bartenders.'

TV and movies are full of bartenders who listen to their customers and offer support and advice. Remember Dwayne, the giant puppet-loving bartender in *Forgetting Sarah Marshall*, who listens patiently to Jason Siegel moan about his broken heart but knows when it's time to give him a little tough love and send him out the door?

Sure, you might not want to take advice from Sam or Woody on *Cheers* or Moe on *The Simpsons*, but they were there to listen when you needed them. And of course, you could always count on *The Love Boat's* Isaac to steer you right.

Q: Did any of your advice blow up in your face?

A: Nope. I'm a pro, buddy.

Q: Eventually, you moved away and couldn't write. Did you have any issues with the Stand-in Bartender?

A: Just his awful writing and his lousy advice and the fact that he called himself, *The Bartender* which might have led people to think I was still writing the column.

Plus, I could be wrong, but I don't believe the Stand-In Bartender had ever tended bar a day in his life, which should be a requirement for someone doling out advice under the name *The Bartender*, I think.

No, honestly, we just had very different writing styles and we approached advice differently... I felt a bit protective of the *Ask the Bartender* column since I'd started it when the Insider first launched, so I was pretty critical when I saw the first few Stand-In columns after I left, but I'm glad there was someone to keep things going.

Long-distance advice isn't quite the same as sitting at the bar and confiding all your problems to the person pouring your drink and *The Bartender* needed to be in Dawson City, even if I couldn't be there anymore.

Q: Your last column appears to be December 1, 1998. The column simply reads — 'The Bartender moved away. We're working on it.' What happened?

A: I did write a few after I left, once I mastered the craft of communicating via email. It was a brave new world. I'm not sure if there was a gap after that issue or if that really was my last column.

Q: Any advice to your readers today?

A: Ha. I'm out of practice. Nope, no advice, just lots of love and good wishes from down south. I miss Dawson City and the amazing people who live there all the time. Hopefully, I'll get back up one of these days and bring my two boys along so they can see all the cool and crazy places where mom used to work.

Q: Do you ever take your own advice?

A: Does a brain surgeon operate on himself? Just kidding. I am great at giving other people advice but not always as great at knowing what I should do when I have a big dilemma.

It's always easier to give advice when you're removed from a situation because I can look at a problem rationally without having a bunch of emotional baggage clouding my judgement... of course, sometimes a situation absolutely requires an emotional response.

I've made my share of mistakes in life, but I've also had a lot of successes along the way, too, and some of those successes wouldn't have happened if I hadn't made a mistake or two.

I'm a lot more comfortable in my own skin now than I was twenty odd years ago when I was writing *Ask the Bartender*. Wow, it's been a long time.

So, yeah, I trust my judgment and am better at listening to my gut than I was back then, but I also have some really thoughtful and amazing friends who I know I can call anytime I could use some advice of my own.

There's nothing wrong with needing an outside perspective from time to time, especially when your own approach to a challenge just doesn't seem to be working. Even a bartender needs advice sometimes.

***

Let's have a peek at some of the best of *Ask the Bartender* from 1998.

Dear Bartender,
My boyfriend broke up with me. What should I do?
Down in the Dumps

Dear Down,
Boy, have you come to the right person! I'm sorry to say I've been in your shoes more often than I'd like.

As a result, I have a sure-fire, self-tested system for putting your self-esteem back together.

Day One: Wallow. Experience self-pity like you've never experienced it before. Scream, punch walls and cry until your face is a blotchy mess.

Do not, under any circumstances, even consider getting dressed or leaving your house. Wrap yourself up in a blanket, park yourself in front of the TV with a pint of Rocky Road and whimper to yourself.

Day Two: Call your girlfriends. Women are great at this stuff. They will immediately show up on your doorstep oozing sympathy and offer supporting hugs.

They will present you with a bottle of wine (or better yet, tequila) and videos of old *Melrose Place* episodes and will sit for hours with you, griping about how all men are bastards and how your boyfriend is an idiot.

Day Three: Your friends will call you and see if you're okay. This is a good time to throw some Visine in your eyes and venture into town to have coffee with one of them. Don't go anywhere your ex might be. You're not ready yet. Think of something he does that really annoyed you and start asking yourself what you ever saw in the jerk.

Day Four: You know that haircut you've been thinking about but didn't get because your boyfriend likes long hair? Go do it.

Hairdressers are great people to be around when you've just been dumped, plus the shock of seeing yourself in the mirror will distract you from thinking about your ex.

Also, go shopping and let the salesgirl talk you into something that looks fabulous on you.

Day Five: Call your friends, get dressed up and hit the town. Everyone will tell you how great you look and will admire how strong you seem.

Your ex might see you. Pay him no mind. Right now, he's beating himself up for having been stupid enough to let a beautiful girl like you slip through his fingers. Hold your head up high and smile. You are on the road to recovery.

Weeks or months later: If your ex comes crawling back, do not even consider it. There's a reason it didn't work out, and remember, this is your one and only chance to reject HIM! Good luck.

Dear Bartender,

My boyfriend sweats so much that after a little make-out session our sheets are soaking wet. It's a little off-putting, but he's really embarrassed about it, so I try not to make a big deal out of it, but enough is enough. Is there anything we can do?

Slipping and Sliding

Dear Slipping,

Try conserving water. A shower à deux combined with a little baby powder might dry things up.

Switch your sheets to one hundred percent cotton and sprinkle a little cornstarch on them. Have an extra set handy. Your boyfriend should also be geared up in cotton clothes and anti-perspirant and should do his best to avoid alcohol, caffeine, cigarettes and spicy food. If this doesn't help, don't despair — a visit to our local medical doctor might help.

Keep in mind that this is not the worst problem in the world. I mean, what's a little sweat between close friends?

Dear Bartender,

A close friend of mine hit on me when we were both really drunk. I didn't do much to fend her off and I really regret it, especially because we're both female and I'm not comfortable with exploring a relationship outside of friendship. Lately, though, she's become very affectionate with me in public and I'm embarrassed because people are starting to talk. How do I let her know I made a mistake without hurting her feelings?

Sorry for Swinging

Dear Sorry,

Treat her the same way you would a guy whose affection you didn't return — with respect. Apologize if she feels you led her on but be clear that you want to keep your relationship a 'friendship only' one. I'm sorry to say her feelings will probably be hurt, but if you don't play games like avoiding her and you continue to treat her with dignity, she'll recover, and you should be able to salvage your friendship.

Dear Bartender,

This may seem petty and self-centred, but is it crazy of me to want to dump my boyfriend for driving a souped-up Camaro and playing air guitar in public?

Humiliated Honey

Dear Humiliated,

Lose him unless you are looking forward to years of Bon Jovi concerts and monster truck rallies.

Chapter 8
The Market Report

Wayne Potoroka leaned over the makeable birdie putt at the Dawson City golf course and said what most writers would never say to their editors: "I thought you were going to be a puff, for sure."

Wayne can say the strangest things. His mind is always somewhere else, digesting endless files at any one moment. Still, this was a strange utterance considering the pressure of the putt; considering that I controlled his content.

We don't have many chances at a six-foot, left-bearing break for glory. We don't have many chances at being a newspaper columnist. He needed to focus.

I was not completely surprised. This was Potoroka, after all. He was one of the Insider's surliest, most inconsistent columnists. He was also by far the most talented.

Today, Wayne is mayor of Dawson City. He began his political career by covering the sewer beat for the Insider.

He defeated Peter Jenkins soundly in a 2012 municipal election. Since then, he has worked to build, then rebuild, the town's sewer plant. He is still on the sewer beat.

Wayne was enthralled that no one actually knew where the waste went in 1998. They probably don't know where it goes today. He wrote article after article about it.

'Somewhere downriver, or maybe upriver — we can't be too sure,' he finally discerned.

"My first job was as a landscaper, but I upped that to digging sewer lines," Wayne had told me about his 1994 arrival into Dawson, just a day or two removed from my own thunderous entrance into town.

We didn't meet in 1994. We didn't meet in 1995, 1996 or even in 1997. Wayne was far too busy digging trenches and evidently his actions were not newsworthy enough to appear on my journalistic radar.

Early in 1998, we had still not met. He had already graced the pages of the Insider a couple of times.

I saw his words in my newspaper one cold January Tuesday while I was in Whitehorse. The Insider was into its eighth month of operation.

In that column, Wayne detailed the simplest thoughts in the most vibrant English. Someone had stolen his snowmobile and he was happy to get it back — in five hundred words.

What the hell is this?

Kim was Wayne's champion. "You'll like Wayne," she kept saying by phone to me in Whitehorse.

Flipside, she was keeping the peace and the home fires burning in Dawson; "You'll like Chris, he's a good editor," she had sucked up to Wayne.

Neither of us had believed her.

"Ya, well I thought you were going to be a complete prick," I retorted, as Wayne concentrated on the putt.

Wayne was still figuring out the break, almost unreadable on Canada's most northern grass greens, which are often broken up by permafrost divots that require careful attention. My comment did nothing to break his concentration. He didn't even lift his head.

When I first read how Wayne had filled a column with a simple, entertaining consideration about his snowmobile, I was impressed.

Nothing happens in Dawson City in January. Absolutely nothing.

Did I want a writer who could fill half a page with nary a thought outside of, 'hey, thanks for returning my sled' and make it sound entertaining and reasonable?

Absolutely.

I was hooked.

I don't recall when we actually met. I don't know why, either. It certainly isn't important to me.

What I do remember were late Saturday nights in 1998, happily alone in the office, putting the Insider to bed while I listened intently to *Finkleman's 45s* on late night CBC public radio.

I was always waiting for Wayne to file.

Wayne was always the last to file his weekly meanderings. He called it the *Market Report*.

While the average drinker in town was glued to *The Bartender*, those in the know were sucked in by the *Market Report*.

Wayne could take English and turn it into a circus freak show. I loved it. So did many others.

The *Market Report* was always worth the wait.

I loved learning the drama that he could conjure from his couch, the bar, the sewage treatment plant or from whomever he met on the street.

Wayne is a chin scratcher, a ponderer, a politician.

He was also a miner, a teacher, a hockey player and everyone's friend. He could talk sewers and people actually listened.

Sometimes, he could even sink a putt.

Ah, the hell with it. Let's let Wayne's words describe themselves, and you can imagine what I felt on Saturday June 30, 1998, as CBC poured out its soul far into the night, and I waited and waited and waited, until I finally received…

The Market Report
By Wayne Potoroka
Look, it's late Saturday night, hours past the time that this was supposed to be in for editing and I'm stuck for anything fresh. It's been a long day, really it has. So, in an attempt to take care of this matter as quickly as

possible, I have dredged up the very first *Market Report* I ever wrote.

Upon completion, it was, for very good reasons, told to fester in the "myfiles" folder of my computer. Since then, it has been very well-behaved and never made much noise of any sort.

Except for now when I look to it for help in my hour of need.

Still, as I read it again, I can't help but think back to this winter when the cold and numbing dim settled in to sit and chat with my mind awhile.

I remember it well. There was lots of hollering and laughing and if I'm not mistaken, cold's half-witted second cousin dropped by with a bottle of whiskey.

Never-the-less, I just want everyone to know I'm feeling much better now, really. And no hard feelings, either.

Pardon me while I pick away at the scab of time and take a peek at the coagulated lesion of a more imprudent period.

If any of us were paying attention a few weeks ago, we would have noticed a rapidly rising film of grease brilliantly ladled (with amorous intent) by the soup spoon of prevarication, quite quickly and efficiently, while standing at the bar of a properly frequented downtown pub.

At first, she wasn't so sure. After all, she had been alerted by her friends that this may not be the utensil for her, but what harm could come from talking, and accepted his offer of a drink.

Never one to retard progress or pass up an opportunity, spoon nimbly polished his tarnished features to a luminous splendour and expertly delivered a stainless-steel presentation that had grease beguiled.

She could feel a lardy exterior soften that gave no offence at all to escorting spoon home on the promise of a nightcap and perhaps some late-night television, but the amber haze of a three a.m. consummation labours hard when properly lubricated, fetching grease long in its grip.

TV remained hushed — liquor stayed out of sight — as spoon gently waltzed grease over to couch who cushioned the impact of their mass.

Watching her inverted reflection disappear, past the supple membrane of her aspect, grease relented to her libidinous desires and spurred spoon on, who surfaced, asked grease to pass his smokes and trundled off to the fridge to see what beer was up to.

Flustered, agitated, and more than just a little disappointed, grease began to rise (couch, always the gentleman, gave her a hand) but was thrown back down by a tightening sensation in her paunch.

She laid there breathless while the late-night silence was interrupted by the hiss and snap of her quickening effervescence, followed by a repulsive pungency that had easy chair in a flap and end table heading for the door.

Couch, now pinned down by grease, would tell the others later of the barely audible baritone growl deep in grease's oily cavity that escalated an octave into a screech until her now vigorously boiling surface ruptured, making wall whimper at the mess (she was always the neat freak in the family).

The commotion proved too much for stand-up lamp, who fainted and would have acquired a nasty lump had not wood stove been there to catch her as he stood gasping at the sight of grease desperately straining to suppress the heaving lump that begged to be belched (but there was no stopping now).

And it was there, in all the turmoil and suet, that grease, speaking with disbelief and embarrassment (this could not be happening to her), rumbled thunderously and begat the three impudent pricks that stole my Skidoo.

One could hardly blame them their ignorance given the exceptional nature of their genesis, so I propose to extend the open hand of harmony.

Drop on by any time and we can hash this thing out.

I've got a plate of smokies put out and your names carved into my chest with a razor blade so don't be so rude and stay awhile.

And now for your market prices...

Lentils up 15 cents,

While peas drop 10.

Hog prices on the way down.

With community values doing much the same.

***

I have dozens of *Market Reports* ready for just this occasion. I had forgotten them all, save for spoon, grease and friends, detailed in full glory above. It was the only one I searched for.

Even today, this may be the best column I have ever read. It simply stuck with me.

Someone else must have thought so, too. Wayne turned his *Market Report* meanderings into a University of Victoria master's degree in journalism in 2006. He still writes, edits and prophesizes to anyone who will listen.

But can he make a birdie putt?

Maybe drop him a line and see if he's up for a game. He might be able to do it again.

Chapter 9
More than just a TV guide

The big blue bin of old Insiders I've carted around contain an original slice of Dawson City's one hundred-twenty-five year history.

I see headlines in these papers I haven't seen anywhere else. No other media outlet picked up these stories, or if they did, we were the first.

Events happen in the Klondike that don't happen anywhere else.

The stories that result from investing time into these events are a product of the area's isolation, climate, environment and the type of people it attracts; adventurers searching for their dreams or escaping their past.

Dawson City is an exciting place. If I am given a choice to write in a big, southern city or Dawson City, well, the Yukon wins hands down every time.

Let's go back to my big blue bin of aging Insiders and have a read.

The front-page headline for July 7, 1997 simply explained: 'Five Bears Shot in West Dawson.'

The story was by Kim Favreau. She had seen a bear trap sitting across the Yukon River at the ferry landing and got curious.

Kim finally had a story she could literally chase and chase she did.

Let's backtrack a little.

West Dawson was once the site of Canada's most amazing summer pilgrimage. It was simply called Tent City.

Do you remember how I was told to camp when I came up for my first summer? I wasn't the only one.

Between 1990 and 2000, thousands of people flocked to Dawson each summer to work, play and stay.

Sometime in this decade, a tent city with over one hundred unofficial sites became the norm.

With the opportunity to freely camp, students and travellers flocked to town in search of work. They all brought boots and tents. The locals called this summer population "transients".

Free camping allowed them to avoid expensive rents, live outside, have a great time and hopefully bank enough money to pay for fall tuition or a winter ticket to Thailand.

With my long hours at work, I did everything I could to avoid Tent City and stay in town. People would be forced to wait at the ferry landing until the old boat arrived, then be carted over to the far bank of the Yukon River. I thought it was a giant waste of time.

The campers were generally left alone by local authorities unless there was a problem. These were rare.

If there was a conflict, it was generally with wildlife.

Unfortunately, these conflicts could be major. Wildlife and humanity are always on a collision course in Canada's gigantic forests that are now riddled with roads.

The campers were attracting the bears.

Yukon Conservation regional manager John Russell spilled the beans to Kim about the bear trap. He was more than happy to get his message out.

"There are two groups. Some people are very good. They are very concerned, clean and use food lockers. Others have no regard at all for bear safety. They store food in their tents and cook in their tents."

We all know this story. It's repeated in Canada each summer. The headlines often talk about a bear encounter. That's right 'a bear.'

One. Not five.

Five. What the hell? In terms of sightings and complaints, the Dawson area was the worst in the Yukon, Russell explained. Considering Yukon's small human population and healthy bear population, that probably made it the worst in Canada.

An entire family — a mother and cubs — had been exterminated by the Yukon government. Someone had to ask some serious questions.

June 28, 1997 was the date of the massacre. Kim found a Tent City dweller that was involved for her front-page story.

"It flipped my tent and slashed the bottom out. It took my pack and dragged it," the camper had told Kim, as she roamed Tent City looking for carnage and the story. The camper was adamant no food was in her tent.

Still, something smelled nice. And it cost a mother and three teenage cubs their lives. A fifth bear had been killed outside of Tent City, near a miner's cabin.

Fortunately, no camper was injured.

Two years later, that injuring attack finally came. A young woman named Carrie was in Tent City when an aggressive black bear tore into her.

That attack signalled the end for Tent City.

The Tr'ondëk Hwëch'in won the land back in its land claim settlement and Tent City was closed down. No one has tented there since.

I turn back to Kim today to recount the tale. She lived in Tent City at one time and remembers it clearly:

"Carrie did survive. A local landscaper, Dave, came to her aid and fought off the bear with a stick. It was gnawing on her leg."

Dave Calnan received high recognition for his efforts. He was awarded the British Stanhope Gold Medal from the Royal Humane Society, the Canadian Governor General's Award for Bravery, the Carnegie Award for Bravery in the United States and the Yukon

Commissioner's Award for an outstanding achievement.

Thanks to Carrie's high level of athleticism and muscle mass, she endured many surgeries but didn't require an amputation, Kim recalled.

"Carrie came back to Dawson the next summer. I remember seeing this girl, who had almost lost her leg, now jogging past me. I cried."

In 2017, I walked around Tent City for old time's sake. I could barely tell that this had once been a bustling community.

Bears and humans were gone. The trails that moved people between all the tents were no longer discernible.

Tent pads and camp spots were swallowed by vegetation. Nature had simply reclaimed the land and with it, all the stories, save this one, have disappeared. It's probably for the best.

Let's dig a little deeper into the big blue bin to find just another slice of Klondike history.

July 14, 1997: The front-page headline screams: 'Bottom Out! Gold Prices Hit Low'.

Boy, did they ever.

Gold value plummeted from approximately five hundred dollars an ounce to under three hundred dollars an ounce in a few weeks. The collapse was astounding, and it had nothing to do with Dawson City. It was the lowest gold price in twelve years.

Kim Favreau once again had the front-page story.

The Euro dollar was being introduced to the world and the countries involved had to back their currency with gold, explained Cory Keller, a local gold buyer.

Other countries followed suit. Australia dumped one hundred and sixty-seven tons of gold onto the market all at once in 1997. That's a lot of gold.

Suddenly, Klondike gold wasn't very valuable, and the miners felt the pinch. So did Dawson City — for ten years.

Gold's value didn't really return until 2008. It sits around two thousand dollars an ounce today. Gold miners are once again getting rich in the Klondike. But in 1997, Dawson City had officially entered into an enormous recession. Many people quit mining, putting a large dent in the Yukon's economy.

Let's turn to page three. Two people had returned home to Dawson that week in very different fashions and had terrific stories to tell.

Bill Bushell had been a new father in 1950. The celebration nearly turned tragic when he personally rescued his wife from the Dawson City hospital that winter. The old wood building caught fire and was burning down at forty below zero.

Someone else had saved Bushell's infant daughter, he explained as he recounted the emotional tale to Kim.

Kim met Bushell at a centennial celebration event and wanted his interview. It was his first time back to town in forty-seven years. What a story.

"It's heart wrenching," he said, standing at the old site. "The hospital was right here."

There was another story on the same page, that same edition, about a guy returning to town.

But Wade Simon's re-entrance attracted much more fanfare than the returning fire-beating father. Simon owned Dawson's busiest restaurant, Klondike Kate's, with his partner Josèe.

Simon mostly ran the morning kitchen while Josèe ran the front end.

The week previous, Simon disappeared from behind the grill. A local RCMP sleuth recognized him from a wanted picture dating back about fifteen years.

It turned out that Simon was actually Phillipe Luc Lamarche, wanted for skipping out of a Quebec halfway house. The law had finally caught up with him.

RCMP officers entered Klondike Kate's kitchen and escorted Lamarche away to jail in Whitehorse. Josèe never had a clue about Simon's past, she had explained to me in detail in the previous week's Insider.

She didn't even know her beloved had another name.

The arrest drew national media attention from the RCMP press release, but the Insider had the scoop. It was awesome.

A local letter-writing campaign ensued in support of Simon's positive stature in the community after my interview with Josèe the week before.

That full-page story in the June 28 edition, our second, spread the word and led to the campaign.

A Whitehorse judge relented, and Simon was released back to serve out his parole in his kitchen in Dawson, as long as he didn't leave town.

In a follow-up article, Simon thanked Dawsonites and explained how he was grateful to finally clear his name and no longer be on the run. Wade was forever Wade with the locals. Like Bushell, it was important for him to be back in town.

This was great journalism: dead bears, selfless heroism, fugitive cooks and crashing economies!

We really were more than a TV guide and we were only a few weeks old. People were picking up the Insider and reading every word.

There was always death in the Insider, it seemed. Newspapers simply search it out — it's their mandate.

And the local rivers provided much of the fodder.

Twenty percent of canoeists end up wet, explained Ron Ryant, who once rented canoes out of the Dawson City Trading Post for daily excursions on the fast flowing, dangerous Klondike River.

Sixty-seven-year-old Dawson resident Fred Chuddy ended up wet, then lost in the Klondike. A week after his disappearance, we reported the RCMP were still searching for him. Fred never turned up. It was sad.

Let's dig deeper into the big blue bin for another river story.

I find a letter from John Cramp, notorious for attending town council meetings and calling out officials on their policies and sub-par practices.

Cramp could rant with the best of them. He lived out of town in Bear Creek. He appreciated and defended his solitude and his right to be left alone.

On July 14, 1998, Cramp filled a full page with that letter. He was upset. His chickens had been killed by a loose dog and that dog had paid for its actions with its life, courtesy of Cramp's shot gun.

Cramp's sadness was evident in his writing, which criticized the town's dog catching practice among other things.

He didn't want to shoot anything, but he did.

Four months later, like the dog, Cramp was dead. Maybe. His empty canoe was found on the shores of the Yukon River. He has never been seen again. The Insider captured it all.

The paper was working. People were dying and people were reading, money was flowing thanks to dozens of advertisements and our stories were leading to changes in the community.

Dawson City finally got a dog catcher and a humane society. The town no longer simply rounded up and shot loose dogs at the end of summer. Conflicts between residents over free-roaming pets slowed dramatically. More stray huskies lived.

Tent City was closed down in 2000 and many bears have since lived long lives in West Dawson.

Wade Simon is a free man, body, soul and mind.

The rivers still claim lives each year, though people are more aware of the dangers.

We were doing everything right by capturing the issues of the day and helping the public to voice their solutions. It was the best of times made by covering the worst of times.

The Insider was booming.

I don't think anybody ever actually used the TV guide.

And the big blue bin I've carted around from place to place for more than twenty years still holds all the stories today.

Chapter 10
No Easy Fixes

CWIB was making a racket.

My only neighbour had found love and was experiencing it in a way that suited her.

It was the middle of June 1997, and my tent was still parked on the shores of the Yukon River after almost two months. I didn't use it much — maybe six hours a night.

This time was just long enough to leave work around midnight most nights, take the kilometre walk 'home' and then attempt to sleep.

After buzzing at work for twelve to fourteen hours a day, it usually took me an hour or two to unwind.

I had little choice but to listen to CWIB make late night love.

I would then wait for her to scream at her man to get out. I would hear him march through the weeds past my tent.

The hair on my neck would stand on end as that man walked by. I could only imagine the man who chose CWIB to be his lover.

Sometimes, I thought I'd rather have taken my chances with the bears in West Dawson than with tenting near CWIB. I always discarded the thought. I hated the ferry.

I needed to get off the ground, literally. This wasn't going to be so easy.

Dawson City was jammed with people. Tent City was full. The campgrounds were full. There was nowhere to rent anywhere, and even if there was, my one hundred dollars a week salary wasn't going to cut it.

My friend Paula once tried to rent me her tool shed for five hundred dollars a month. I almost took it.

The work orders were incessant. The lifestyle was extreme. We do what we must do to get a story and catch some sleep.

The grind was starting to wear. I'd been living out of the same backpack for two years. Work was intense. The deadline pressure was enormous.

And CWIB was getting loud and agitated.

I mentioned my homelessness situation to Zig.

"There's a camper in Lousetown I know about. It's just parked. Nobody is using it," he said.

"A camper?"

"Yes."

"What the hell?" I said that a lot, it seems. It was becoming a theme.

"It's free. It belongs to someone I know. You can use it."

My eyes opened wide with surprise. Why hadn't he mentioned this in the last month?

Oh well.

We drove out to my tent and picked it up. I remember we were so busy we didn't even take the time to dismantle it. We simply put the whole thing in the back of Zig's truck and drove it out to Lousetown, about two kilometres south of Dawson City.

Lousetown got its name because it was the Klondike's industrial hotbed and housed the local ladies of the night back at the turn of the century. The girls had caused a couple of bad fires in the town's early years and had been relegated to the suburbs.

There were no girls there now; just a twenty-year-old deserted camper lying in the weeds. It was to be my home. Kind of. It had no key and no amenities. It was yellowing and dusty. It looked abandoned because it was. At least the bears couldn't bite through it. At least CWIB was far away. I stuffed my tent inside the unlocked door and went back to work.

It's impossible to remember all the stories that we published from 1997–1999.

In total, we created seventy-nine issues of the Dawson City Insider. I was responsible for all of them. I never missed a deadline. Today, sixty-one of those issues remain safe in my big blue bin. The others are missing.

If you have a few old Insiders around, and you happen to read this, drop me a line. I'd love to fill in the collection.

Like I said, I can't remember most of the stories.

When I started this book project, an idea would strike me, and I'd go to the big blue bin and try to find the paper that held the story that would enforce the idea shaping inside of me. It was a painful process. I'd have to guess the year of that issue, then the month, the page, etcetera, until I found it.

Stupid waste of time.

So, I went through all the papers one day and inventoried every story, editorial, column and letter. There are thousands of pieces of information.

When I peruse the list now, so many hair-raising stories come rushing back.

I wrote about Dawson City as a stringer for the *Yukon News*, *The Globe and Mail*, the *New York Times* and CBC for a decade after the Insider was long laid to rest. I covered many incredible stories in Yukon and Alaska. But the following story has always stood out. It never repeated itself. Not anywhere.

Aedes Scheer is a phenomenon. She was raised on a farm near Strathmore, Alberta and found herself living in Dawson City after partnering with a German dentist who practiced out of his home and built planes in his front yard.

When the relationship ended, Aedes stayed.

She worked as the closest thing central Yukon had as a veterinarian in those years. She was a tech with a two-year diploma. She is now a medical doctor.

One day, she stopped by the office and said she had a story to share. Aedes is intelligent and well-spoken. I listened. Her story was so amazing I had her write it out. I didn't want to taint her intelligent and accurate words.

Those words are still caught in time, stored safely in my big blue bin.

Let's go back to July 7, 1997.

**

Emu Attacked

By Aedes Scheer

The evening of November 30, 1996, I received a radio phone call from Diana Deren. Ernie the Emu had been attacked by a dog and was in bad shape. I had never seen an emu before, let alone worked on one, so I called a veterinarian in Whitehorse for suggestions. He also had never worked on such a bird and referred me to a vet in Calgary. When I finally spoke with her, I explained that it was minus forty-something outside, the bird was several miles downriver and I would be traveling by snow machine to reach it.

I was not a veterinarian but an independent vet tech, and could she recommend an anaesthetic and antibiotic dosage? She said she could not comply with my request and that the bird should be taken to Whitehorse immediately. I paused, thought for a moment that perhaps she had not heard me and said again, 'It is below minus forty, the closest vet is over five hundred kilometres away. I would like to know what drugs I can

127

use because I am going down there anyhow. Can you help me?'

All she offered was to use a local anaesthetic. The next morning, Ron arrived to pick me up and I opted to take all my clinic supplies I could take with me. Just in case.

Once we arrived, Diana and I sat down with the *Emu Farmer's Handbook* to become more acquainted with the particulars of emu anatomy and anything else I could glean from those pages. After a coffee, we went to have a look.

It became immediately apparent that a local anaesthetic was not going to be of much use.

A flap of skin and muscle the length of Ernie's amazingly long neck dangled from the base of his beak. His windpipe had been torn and his breathing ragged. All that remained of his hind end was chewed, bleeding muscle, tail and pelvic bones and the cloaca (like the human rectum).

Inside my head, a little voice started to exclaim, 'god oh god oh god oh god…'

So, I turned to my bags and drew up a hefty dose of anaesthetic. I said to Ernie, "Okay, bird, today you are a 70-pound dog," and injected the drug into his thigh muscle.

Within a few minutes, he came crashing down but not before vomiting his recent meal all over Diana and I.

She and I looked at each other and realized that half of this had sprayed through a multitude of tooth holes in his oesophagus.

If this had not happened, it would have been very difficult to find these, but now vomit clearly marked each of these holes. This was becoming a bigger task by the minute.

Tommy Taylor had arrived and was holding Ernie in place. With Diana handing me suture material and gauze, we worked for several hours on a tarp on the barn floor by the light of flashlight and kerosene, cutting away the dead tissue, piercing together the good. It worked and was hard work.

As testament to the toughness of these birds and diligence of Ron and Diana, seven weeks later it was nearly impossible to find my suture lines or scars on Ernie. He experienced somewhat of a temporary setback in his growth development but is alive and well today.

I am reminded that we are often capable of more than we are willing to credit ourselves. You just never know until you throw yourself into a situation and put it to the test.

***

I think that last paragraph is what seared that story into my brain. Until I read it just now, I hadn't realized why it was important to me. The emu-saving story at forty below with no electricity, no running water and limited knowledge is incredible.

I had my own battles and solutions to think about and one solution presented itself just when I needed it: the tabloid printer finally arrived!

I had followed the same route three weeks in a row: finish the paper then drive to Whitehorse, find elbow room at the *Yukon News*, fix files, install fonts on the office computer and print out the pages to prepare for the press.

But with the new printer, I could change my schedule. I could lighten my heavy load, and I did.

During my last production run to Whitehorse, a cop pulled me over at the exit from the Pelly Crossing gas station, about one hundred and eighty-five kilometres south of Dawson, because I'd failed to come to a complete stop upon entering the deserted highway.

There were no vehicles on the road except for his and mine. I lost it on him. I had hit the end of my tether. Screaming at bored RCMP officers is never a good idea. He ticketed me, of course. The Insider was starting to cost me money. This process had to change.

So, I was jubilant when the delivery truck dropped off the new printer. No more driving. No more tickets.

Zig was also pleased. He loved new toys. I simply loved the paper.

This toy was special, though. It would allow us to print pages in tabloid format — the same size as our newspaper. It was amazing!

After the printer arrived, I no longer had to make the long trip to Whitehorse. I drove the company truck to the Air North office in Dawson and made sure the boards were on the flight to Whitehorse. It was a far shorter trip.

The boards would get delivered to the *Yukon News* and printed the next day. Air North would then ship the new edition back north and I would deliver it around town. In exchange, we gave Air North a free ad in the paper.

It was a good trade. It was a good schedule. It saved me a lot of driving.

Then I would take the rest of Sunday off to walk, rest and eat.

The tabloid printer made all the difference. Unfortunately, we didn't really know how to use it, and many hours of production time were lost before we finally figured it out.

Computer memory in those days was tiny. We are talking about single digits of megabytes available for RAM. Not thousands. The term gigabyte was not even on our radar yet. I think the Apple Macintosh Power PC memory was eventually doubled up to hold four megabytes of RAM, maybe eight.

The printer could hold two.

Every page of the Insider had hundreds of pieces of information — logos encapsulated in advertisements, photos, words, clip art and fonts.

They all had to be brought into several programs, then imported onto the page. The page was then saved, then all the pages saved as one big file.

This was a challenge to the technology of the day. Digital files were possible, but the process was certainly hiccupy.

Links to files would be broken inexplicably. Pictures would come out far too pixelated. Fonts would never be found.

Every problem had to be fixed individually or the paper wouldn't print as it should.

I remember using the printer for the first time. We downloaded a page from the Insider to print. The printer received the file then blinked. It blinked again. And again. And again. It didn't stop blinking.

The page was downloading to the printer ever-so-slowly, one file, one font, one letter at a time. It was excruciating. Half an hour later, the page finally printed. I caught an error. I fixed the error and reprinted. I waited again.

I did the math. The paper was sixteen pages. That meant a minimum eight hours to print. It was quicker to drive to Whitehorse.

Why can nothing ever be easy?

I remember finishing production one Saturday night in July 1997, stuck in the Klassic, Dom and the tenants trying to sleep. Zig was on the road. Kim had been sent home hours earlier.

I watched the printer blink all night.

I finally had all sixteen pages printed around five a.m. The process was frustrating. I thought the printer would save me time. It didn't.

It was weeks before we fixed this issue. It was a remarkably easy solution.

There was a PageMaker drop down menu command to overcome this problem: 'capture files to print.' That's all I had to select to cut the printer time down from a half an hour a page to three minutes. We could have saved dozens of hours if only we'd known about this basic command. So learning goes. This was the downfall of using mostly keyboard short cuts – we rarely went to the drop-down menus, so we didn't see this option.

The fix was simple, but the irritation lingered. I was still mad at the waste of time. I buried my weeks of built up frustration and kept working. There was work to do. There was always work to do. Don't look back.

With little money, no home but an abandoned camper with no heat, outhouse or water, and working far beyond my means, well, the lifestyle was continuing to affect me.

I was smoking more and started to drink coffee. I wasn't eating. I wasn't sleeping. I had no fixed address. I had no contact with anything from my past except for the student loan guy, who found me through the business.

But each morning, I would begin anew. I was optimistic and I loved the experience. Then each late

133

night, I would return to my abandoned camper in the woods exhausted, alone and hungry. I had very little to be passionate about except for the Insider. And I loved it.

I found the motivation to keep going, relishing the daily unforeseen problems and adventures while ignoring my own well-being. Problems meant opportunities to grow and succeed.

It was important to try, like Aedes.

Chapter 11
Business, Not Usual

The first time I met Chera (pronounced share-ah), she was standing on her head in the corner of our office.

She was making noises: Beeeeeeep. Bwaaaaaaaaaaa. Dooo Deeee Doooo. Miiiiiiiingggg.

I was wondering if she was trying to mimic the sound of the dial-up internet modem connecting. She wasn't. She was probably just thinking about something out loud.

Chera had driven north that summer to be with her boyfriend and look for work. She didn't have a resume. She didn't have any experience. She didn't know how to use a computer. She didn't offer much of anything, really.

But she was standing on her head.

Zig knew her from previous summers. Chera was a good friend so he hired her to sell and build advertising for the *Yukon Miner's Directory*, a contract he'd picked up from the Yukon Chamber of Mines.

The *Miners' Directory* was a one hundred-plus page book published annually. It would take months to build. The advertising in it was worth a fortune.

But someone had to contact every mining supply company in the Yukon to sell and/or renew their ad to make it worth anything. That someone was going to be Chera.

I was too busy and wasn't interested in miners nor their directory. Chera was.

Zig was always amazing at giving people a chance. He still is. He can be remarkably generous.

When Chera stopped being upside down, her hair didn't. It continued to stand on end. She was a little ruffled. A little dusty. She looked like she'd just walked out of a gold mine. And she beeped sometimes. She hasn't changed a bit.

People were walking in the door every day looking for work. Some stayed and helped, some moved on. Some just weren't right. Chera was perfect.

I'm really glad Zig hired Chera. She became the Insider's first graphic artist. We shared an office again years later, when I worked as a freelancer covering all things Yukon and she continued to offer graphic design services long after the Insider was laid to rest.

In the summer of 1997, we had to first teach her how to turn on the computer. Chera then took care of the rest. She didn't need any support. She was the support.

The Insider continued to grow. People wanted to write. I trained at least six transients how to be reporters that summer.

Editing their work was a true challenge. Some became columnists and stuck it out for the entire seventy-nine issues that we built. Some just disappeared.

John Wierda was an accredited financial wizard in town and was happy to trade a weekly column for a free advertisement.

He called it *Making Sense of Your Money*. John had figured out the internet and email. He lived in town but only came to the office once, I believe, in two years. He simply emailed in his column and ran the same ad week after week.

John had figured out in 1997 what the rest of the world was just signing up for — the ease of digital transmission of information and how to use it to build a business.

I would load up Netscape Navigator, make sure the modem cord was plugged into the wall and then hit connect. The modem would go through its awful racket. Emails would slowly enter an inbox. Spam was already starting to rear its ugly head. Ugh.

John's column would arrive days ahead of deadline. What Wayne Potoroka offered me through his *Market Report*, John Wierda gave me the opposite.

He was the money guy. I could trust him to come through on time each week. We like that in our money guys.

I didn't have any extra money in those days, so I didn't really think much about his words. It would be interesting to read all his columns again and see if his financial advice was worthy.

They were all directed at the baby boomers. They were the only ones with any money.

Would we all be rich today if we'd followed John's advice? Was John truly a financial wizard? Maybe. Let's have a read from October 1997:

Making Sense of Your Money

By John Wierda

I've decided we need a short break from our assessment of risks inherent in various investments. This week, I want to pass on some tips and other bits of information which may be useful to you in making financial plans.

Changes to the taxation legislation require those people who turn 69, 70 or 71 this year to convert their RRSPs into RRIFs or some other kind of income generating assets.

The conversion must be made on or before December 31 this year. This means your financial advisor, if you have one, or financial institution, will be extremely busy in December.

The decisions you make could affect your income and tax treatment of that income for the rest of your life. Do not leave this decision to the last minute.

Advisors want to provide the best service possible, but we are human. If extremely busy, we may miss something important to you as an individual.

My advice is to sit with your advisor, make an informed decision now and implement prior to December 31.

Research has uncovered a number of interesting facts which, when combined and considered as a whole, may have a dramatic impact on your ability to meet financial goals.

These facts are:

- a higher percentage of births (42.6%) are by women 30 and older.
- children are waiting longer before leaving home and often returning after they have left for a period of time. Most do not pay rent.
- Up to 40% of Canadian families are taking care of older family members.
- Canadians, on average, are now living five years longer than they were 25 years ago. What could this mean to you as a typical baby boomer?

There is a good chance that you may be trying to prepare for retirement while also looking after aging parents, paying for children's post-secondary education and dealing with adult children still living at home.

And you'll need money for retirement because you will probably live longer. This could prove to be financially challenging.

***

Megan à la Mode was our fashion writer. She wrote a column called the *Fashion Eater*. She was also pretty consistent.

Let me explain something first: Dawson City and fashion go together like Paris and modelling. It is a thing. It may not be on TV, it may not involve catwalks, but it's a thing.

There was only one clothing store in town those days — The Raven's Nook, unless residents included the army surplus wear at The Trading Post, which I sometimes did. Megan did as well.

The Raven's Nook offered a range of clothes for everyone: all sizes, all ages, all needs. It made sense. Dawson is far too small to offer fashion to a niche market.

The closest shopping mall was in Vancouver, about three thousand kilometres south. Shopping online in 1997? Forget about it. Amazon was still years away.

As I've mentioned, many transients arrived each summer to work and play in and around town. They brought whatever clothes they could throw in a pack and that was it.

If they got hired as a waiter and required black and whites, then it was up to them to get the necessary outfit.

A pair of black pants could be traded from person to person several times in one summer. There were just no other options.

I had learned to stuff a pair of black pants deep into my pack wherever I went, just in case.

There were only two other reasonable options for expanding wardrobes in Dawson: heading to the Anglican church thrift store or the free store at the dump. Both were extremely effective at clothing people in immediate need.

Deciphering some of the remarkable fashion choices people made, well, that was the stuff of Megan à la Mode's columns. Summer transients sported the hipster look that was still fifteen years away. Megan saw it coming and let readers know.

She was fresh out of fashion design school and loved Dawson City. She has since settled on a small property near the Klondike River to raise a family and sew.

Megan even opened her own winter clothing line and at one time was selling Yukon-made parkas around the world. She's a talented go-getter.

Let's have a read from February 10, 1998:

The Fashion Eater

By Megan à la Mode

Wowee! It's warm, sometimes sunny, the days are getting longer and I'm feeling fashionably carefree! Yup, it's time to reorganize my winter wardrobe in anticipation for spring.

First, a search for new boots! I've cast off my downtrodden and cumbersome Sorrels (although recently advertised in Vogue) for a boot to liberate me!

Well, it's Friday night — to The Pit! What's this!!?

The Pointer Brothers with Disco Joe, shakin' their booty like Bootsy Collins, funky, funky, funky. Yeah, that's it. I want some funky boots to shake, rather, to funky stomp in!

The next afternoon... To the Raven's Nook I go. Oooooo, a pair of Buffalo flared-leg cords hangin' there, just calling my name! A perfect fit. An easily justified tangent, as new boots always need new pants to make a fashion statement.

But I still need new boots. I can't flaunt these flares tucked into a pair of knee-high sorrels. What's a girl to do?

Hmmmm. To the Trading Post! Holy cow, lots of antiques and treasures. And boots! The boots of my dreams: second hand, two-tone green Vietnam jungle boots, already broken in. Oh boy, my flares sway sooo perfectly over them!

Mission accomplished: new jungle boots, new flared cords and the tight striped sweater I bought at the thrift store. I've got new style, and style's gotta be seen!

Where to be seen in Dawson? Riverwest, eating the most fashionable soup in town — carrot ginger. Mmmmm, mouth full, can't talk.

Now playing:

Vietnam jungle boots, Dawson City Trading Post $30.

Buffalo Jeans flared leg cords, Raven's Nook $68.

Striped knit sweater, bag-a-bargain thrift store $2.

Wet and Wild Blueberry Bop nail polish, Ray of Sunshine $3.

***

What would a TV guide be without a TV columnist? And we had one! Pepper Dufresne to the rescue. We almost all watched at least a little TV back then, so let's take a trip down memory lane from November 18, 1997.

Pepper Sounds off on Celine
By Pepper Dufresne

Come on, out with it. Who else had a cheese-o-rama fest last week and hollered at the record-holding, longest-advertised CBC special, *Celine Dion — The Concert*?

Celine's stardom baffles me. I find her to be one of the most irritating people to strut this earth — right up there with the Spice Girls. In an unofficial poll I conducted, most people (99%) expressed similar opinions.

One Dawsonite exasperatingly exclaimed: "Why doesn't she get plastic surgery and change that annoying face? She's got enough money!" Just a wee bit harsh!

If she unnerves me (and others) so much, why do we watch her?

Is it because it's fascinating to watch a person whose wavelength we'll never quite grasp? It's a hoot

143

to make fun of someone who's so cockily confident and yet so tacky. She's got so many snazzy outfits.

It's Sunday in November in Dawson. Is doing something requiring cerebral activity as alien a concept as Celine is to us?

Clad in sculpted garments which revealed parts of her anatomy that I thought only her doctor and hubby should see, Celine entertained a mesmerized crowd with her numerous AM radio hits.

Her painful rendition of the Beatles *Twist and Shout* launched the crowd into a pulsating frenzy. She then fancied herself a jazz singer and started scatting madly, never losing her self-deprecating sense of humour.

Celine was rockin' and kept saying, "I love you, you're the best. I don't want to go home." This is when I responded, "I wouldn't either if I was married to that guy!"

For those of you who don't keep up with Cel, she married her 55-year-old manager in a modest ceremony (hee, hee) a few years back.

This Canadian rocker (she's so electric, I wish she'd do an unplugged album) concluded the evening with *Because You Loved Me*, her sappy hit from the equally saccharine movie *Up Close and Personal*.

This is where I must come clean. In my sentimental Air Supply-type moments, I groove to *Because You Loved Me* and I sang it for the rest of the night.

***

The Insider was getting a little easier each week to fill. I had had my early problems. What start up weekly newspaper in the far north doesn't?

One artist was so offended by the business profile a transient writer wrote about her that she removed as many papers from around town as she could. There was nothing I could do about it. These things happen.

Other writers would commit, stay a week for the free beer, then be gone. But most simply just kept writing for the glory.

Remember, this is long before Facebook; long before people considered having an online presence or an audience. Print was the most powerful tool for spreading an everlasting word. As I look at these aging papers here today and remember how much everyone pretended to hate Celine in 1997, I think it probably still is.

Life was starting to settle for me. No bears attacked the camper I was squatting in. I was managing to find a meal a day. I was adjusting to six hours of sleep a night. I was settling in. I didn't mind my forest quiet.

Then an opportunity came around. It's good to have friends.

Jay Armitage is Dawson City's favorite photographer and historian. He's been capturing imagery from the Klondike since he arrived in the late

1980s. As a long-time Parks Canada tour guide, Jay knows his Yukon history.

Jay was one of the Insider's biggest fans and he had a real home!

He had rented a beat up three-bedroom mobile for the summer in Dawson's south end. Only two of the rooms had been rented.

Jay offered the third room to me for about two hundred fifty dollars a month. Rent would be about sixty-five percent of my money. It was worth it. I jumped at the chance.

When I moved in, I noticed there was a small camping trailer parked in the front yard of the mobile home. It was a trailer renting out space to another trailer. I loved it.

What's this? I asked Jay.

"That's just D's trailer," he said.

Jay explained how he'd rented the front yard out to D so she could park her camping trailer in town. She could use Jay's bathroom and kitchen and still have privacy in her little home.

I had met D once or twice. I laughed at the set up and didn't think much else of it.

I went inside Jay's place and checked it out. It was fine; 1970s vintage everything except for the meanest looking dog I'd ever seen standing fully erect on the couch.

The dog looked like a cross between a barrel-shaped blue heeler and a coyote (it was). It was staring out the window, angry because another dog was having a good time. Its hackles were raised. It was growling low and deep. The dog was going to attack through the window.

Who's this? I asked Jay.

"That's Django," Jay said. "She's D's dog."

Jay didn't say not to worry about Django. Nor did he say she's fine. He said nothing. We both left Django alone.

There was also a beautiful, twenty-something, blonde woman sitting in a chair in a bikini. Her legs were wide open. She was eating raw macaroni out of a box, one dried noodle at a time. It was impossible not to notice her.

I said hi, she said hi back. She crunched when she talked. She never bothered crossing her legs.

Jay told me she rented the other room and had come up to work as a dancer. That dream had mostly failed, and she was working part-time retail around town. She only stayed a few weeks.

My room was dry. There was a real bed. I didn't have to sleep on the forest floor anymore. I had water, laundry, electricity and a stove. I had the Yukon's meanest dog for protection. There was a beautiful blonde in a bikini with little sense of modesty in the living room. Things were looking up.

Thank you, Jay.

Chapter 12
The Village Everitt

This story has been tickling me in that soft place between my lowest rib and my right femur since we covered it back in 1997.

It still makes me smile.

Glen Everitt was pushing a cart full of vegetables across the sloping, cramped floor of Dawson City's General Store when I first met him.

He was a father, an elected town councillor and a grocery clerk. He'd been in Dawson for a while.

By 1996, his sights were set on a much bigger prize than pushing tomatoes: he wanted to be the mayor of Dawson City.

I don't know how he did it, but Glen won that election and remained Dawson's mayor until 2004. His mixed legacy on the town remains today.

Let's again turn back the clock to 1997.

I was just getting my feet wet in the murky puddle that was Dawson City's politics.

Peter Jenkins was gone from municipal government. He had jumped to Yukon territorial politics and was now the representative for the Klondike in Whitehorse. This left a hole in the town's municipal leadership.

Peter was famous for driving the Klondike highway several times a week for the next ten years. I lost count of how many times I passed him on the highway as I recall my own adventures up and down that lonely, dangerous stretch of road.

He remained the elected member of the Legislative Assembly for the Klondike until 2006.

Peter served as mayor again from 2009–12 before he was soundly defeated by Wayne Potoroka, who remains mayor at the time of writing this story. Peter has returned to his office in the Eldorado Hotel.

In 1997, Peter and Glen were not friends. Glen had served on Peter's town council, but his opinion was dismissed at every turn.

They battled at meetings. Glen didn't care. Nor did Peter. They were neither frenemies nor political adversaries. They simply disliked each other.

It was easy to pick up on the animosity, which was great for newspapering. Glen used to complain about Peter relentlessly. Peter just stayed quiet — mostly.

By August 1997, Kim and I had the Insider figured out. We were able to compile up to ten stories on time each week. We had a solid stable of writers. Chera was now helping with all the ad changes. The August 4, 1997 issue had thirty-five ads. Each one had to be created, then either faxed or walked over to the advertiser for further changes or approval. It was a long, tedious process.

Kim and I were responsible for filling in that ever-so-important white space between the ads. It was plenty of work for two of us.

Glen helped make that work easier.

We started to venture deeper into covering tough stories. It was time to start scratching at Dawson's soft underbelly — town council. I found there was plenty to scratch.

Glen wanted expensive improvements to the town. He also wanted to be heard.

Peter didn't like to spend money needlessly and he didn't like reporters asking him to explain his decisions.

While Peter stared down each new journalist that arrived in the Yukon, stoking the fire for the eventual nightmares that would build in their psyches for daring to question him, Glen was the polar opposite. He loved every microphone or tape recorder that was pointed his way. He also loved to spend money.

For the next eight years, I loved pointing it out.

Until 2004, when Glen and his council were overthrown in disgrace by Peter and the Yukon government after the municipality fell into bankruptcy, he never disappointed me.

Glen was eventually convicted in court for misappropriating exactly thirty-eight thousand five hundred dollars in town money for personal use. The town remained millions of dollars in debt for years, until the Yukon government eventually bailed it out.

Kim wandered over to town hall to listen to the weekly council meeting for that August 4th issue.

Glen was announcing to his council, and to the few people in the gallery, that he was about to bill British Columbia premier Glen Clark one hundred thousand dollars through a carefully worded letter.

Hello, sexy story.

Dawson City's mayor was personally dropping that hefty bill on BC's most powerful politician.

There had been a skirmish just north of Prince Rupert, where the Alaska state ferry passes from US protected waters into Canadian waters.

BC fishers had blocked the ferry's route in protest of Alaskan overfishing of the returning salmon stock.

The ferry ran from Skagway, on the Alaskan panhandle, to Prince Rupert. There, it would pick up folks and transport them north to Skagway, where they would depart and continue their long journey to the Yukon and inland Alaska.

However, most visitors to the Yukon never take a ferry. They drive the Alaska Highway.

Only about ten percent of all Alaska Highway travellers even bother with Dawson City, choosing instead to remain on the main road and not turn north to the Klondike. Anchorage and Fairbanks, Alaska are far more attractive to the highway's mostly American tourists.

In the letter, Everitt wrote that Clark was supporting the coastal blockade, which resulted in the suspension of this ferry service. Everitt believed this political action was harming the local economy, even though the blockade only affected a very small percentage of people trying to reach the Klondike.

Everitt demanded compensation from the BC government for Dawson's supposed lost tourism dollars. He also wanted Dawsonites to know that he was doing something to get their money back.

So, he sent Premier Clark a bill.

Media from across Canada caught wind of the story and bombarded Everitt with interview requests.

Kim, once again, scooped the story for the Insider. She was the first to get the letter, prompting the front-page headline 'Dawson Bill Provokes Premier Reaction', after Everitt sprang it onto the public at a weekly council meeting.

"How a premier can sit back and support an action that has cost businesses in British Columbia, Alaska and the Yukon hundreds of thousands of dollars is beyond me. You, and you alone, have created an anger that will hurt and haunt the BC and Yukon economy for years to come," Everitt wrote in his letter to Clark.

The BC Premier refused to consider Everitt's bill. Clark responded publicly to a TV audience of millions across the province. He accused Yukon of taking Alaska's side in the long running salmon dispute.

Clark disagreed that the issue was damaging Yukon's tourism industry.

"The Yukon has a closer relationship with Alaska. There is more sympathy in certain quarters," he said.

Everitt said if the town received the money then it would be 'distributed equitably'.

I considered the issue for several days before penning an editorial.

I believed Everitt's response to be outrageous, even unfathomable. It made zero sense. It was a political move to gain attention and nothing more.

I had never seen a greater attempt at grandstanding by a local politician, and I let Insider readers know how I felt.

Let me backtrack a little.

I believed that a newspaper was not complete unless it had an editorial. The Insider had to take a weekly stand on an issue affecting the town.

The editorial is a reason people read newspapers. Readers may yell, clap or gossip, especially in small towns, where a spicy editorial can sway public opinion dramatically.

I hated writing editorials and it showed.

My editorials were pretty weak. By nature, I'm not confrontational. I like pulling out a good story, but I don't like grilling somebody after they decide they will talk to me.

I'm terrible at taking sides. I like balance. Taking a stand is not my thing.

So, I always left the Insider editorial, *An Insider's View*, until the very end of the weekly production.

Then I would write to fill the hole, which means to write enough words to fill in the space left between the ads, photos or other stories. I always hoped that this hole would be small.

I once wrote that people shouldn't feed the bears, or they could end up attacked in their tents.

I also wrote that renewed infrastructure is good for the town.

Supporting youth was also another weak stance.

You get the point.

But this issue, this little bill sent down to the good folks in BC by our mayor, well, I couldn't let it go.

I even had local summer guy Adam Larson draw up an editorial cartoon. It involved Clark opening his morning mail and finding a bill sent by the mayor of Dawson City. The cartoon was great.

I chose my words carefully. Even if BC did pay the bill, I couldn't see how billing the BC premier was going to solve Dawson's economic woes. It would only help Everitt's publicity.

I let people know how I felt through that week's editorial.

An Insider's View

By Chris Beacom

It's a big bill for a small town — $100,000 to be divided equitably between Klondike businesses. This poses a myriad of interesting questions.

Does the money get split between only businesses related to tourism? Does it go to all businesses in the area?

Does the Trading Post receive as much money as Diamond Tooth Gertie's (casino)? Both businesses cater to tourists and both have potentially lost revenue because of the Alaska ferry/salmon scandal.

Would Darrel Lind receive a couple of thousand bucks or just enough to buy some of his Claim Post fries?

Personally, I'm a little confused. This newspaper is picked up my many tourists every week. We sure could use a new printer. Maybe Colm could use a new hot dog cart.

Say there are 100 businesses in Dawson. If Clark pays his tab, each business could receive $1,000.

This could pay about a week's wages for an employee or two. It could help this year's sluggish economy.

No question, the honourable Mr. Everitt has his heart in the right place. He's concerned about lost business revenue all around, not just that resulting from BC's political decisions.

Everitt says this is not a media ploy, but a legitimate concern. Regardless, he has had media calls from across Canada, the southern US and Europe.

Even if he doesn't want media attention, he's getting it.

And remember, there's no such thing as bad publicity. Any political act that keeps a town of 2,000 people in the international media eye is a positive business move, whether we ever see a penny from Mr. Clark or not.

***

Dawson City never did receive payment.

Clark, obviously, never paid his bill. I don't imagine anyone ever expected that he would.

Harmless grandstanding, perhaps. Still, it was a wingnut move, done unilaterally by Everitt without first contacting his fellow council members or the public.

I decided I'd keep a close watch on our fast and loose mayor. An election was approaching.

There was money to be spent. There was money to be made.

Chapter 13
Money and More

Zig was getting restless.

The Insider was making money. Desktop publishing was making money. Other publications he had on the go were making money. The photocopier was making money. Renters were paying his mortgage.

All could have been fine in Zig's world. It wasn't. He wanted more.

By September 1997, we were starting to plan our winter.

Dawson dries up like all tourist towns in September. The north wind starts to blow. Frost arrives. Leaves fall, people vanish. Forty below soon follows. It's the natural order of life in most of Canada.

I could feel the winds whipping through my trailer bedroom. I had until the end of September to clear out. The owners were not going to keep it habitable through the long, cold winter months.

I was worried, again.

I didn't know where I was going to live as of October 1. I didn't have any money. I didn't have a car. I didn't have anything.

I had the Insider but many of the businesses that supported it through advertising were shutting down for the long winter.

Zig and Josh were hatching a plan to save us all.

I now knew who Josh was. If you recall, I had sort of met him the first day I arrived at the Klassic back in May. He was the guy who told me that Zig would be back later. He didn't say much that day but had a great horned-rim glasses look. Josh was also a fantastic cigarette smoker.

Zig hired him maybe another day or two that summer to "clean up some files" on the office computer, Zig told me.

I didn't know what that meant. Zig was completely in charge of the finances, though I was an unofficial partner. If Zig said he needed Josh to work, so be it. I trusted him.

Josh came and went from the Klassic inconsistently through the summer. He was an opportunist and knew there was money around. He never said anything to me about his work. I just accepted his sporadic presence. I was too busy to give Josh much thought.

The *Yukon News* was printing the Insider in Whitehorse each week. Zig was down there a lot.

He was selling advertising for a widely distributed tourism publication he had operated and published annually for years.

Zig had lots of reasons to visit Steve Robertson, owner of the *Yukon News*. They knew each other well.

The evolution of cable television was causing Steve a dilemma.

Every Friday, Steve would publish the TV guide. He sold it as part of the *Yukon News*, which retailed for a dollar. This had gone on for years. Television, which was completely analogue back then, was no more than a handful of channels offered through a standard cable package.

This was about to change. Whitehorse TV was expanding its channel selections as all cable companies were doing so at that time. Technology improvements were allowing for more choice for viewers. The days of cable television packages had arrived.

This expansion was not good for the *Yukon News*. Printing an expanded TV guide would result in a financial loss. Steve could barely sell enough advertising to cover the cost of printing the current listings. The TV guide was a cost that Steve swallowed for the benefit of his readers – there was no other TV guide option in Whitehorse.

When Steve learned that the listings were going to expand dramatically, he wanted out.

Zig was a natural solution. He and Steve started to talk in September 1997.

By the end of the month, a deal was in place.

Zig acquired the rights to publish Whitehorse' television listings from the *Yukon News* beginning in January 1998.

Zig was thrilled with the success we had found in Dawson with the Insider. He believed copying the model in Whitehorse was a no-fail opportunity. He could expand the business to Whitehorse and cover the costs of the Insider's lost revenue, which was about to dry up with the onset of winter.

A deal was done with Steve before I knew it. Zig would start up a new entertainment newspaper centred around the TV listings and the *Yukon News* would print it. We would pay for both the listings and the printing.

Looking back now, it was a dream deal for Steve. He didn't have to expand his Friday paper. He didn't have to devote human resources to trying to sell additional advertising.

He only had to hand over the rights to the listings to Zig and then bill him for printing the paper each week. Steve wasn't afraid of competing for advertising dollars with Zig. He already owned the town.

Zig was ecstatic. Whitehorse is ten times the size of Dawson and has substantially more money for advertising. If he could convince advertisers how important the expanded TV guide was to the Whitehorse public, he could make a killing.

Josh thought so, too.

I wasn't so sure. Nobody had ever told me how excited they were about the TV guide we published in the Insider each week in Dawson City. Nobody.

Still, I couldn't help but let Zig's exuberance wear off on me. I had no idea where I was going to live that autumn and I also believed our revenue was going to dry up in winter, though I had never spent a winter in the Klondike. I let the idea snowball.

Josh was next to Zig every step of the way. He was a transient guy from Saskatchewan who had spent a couple of summers in town. He did nothing consistent, floating from one short-term job to the next. He was in the bar a lot. He was in his early twenties and was having a good time. I had nothing against him. I also had nothing for him. But I was an optimist, and he was willing to try.

Zig made Josh the Whitehorse sales manager. They worked quickly at finding an office space. To save money, they believed that renting a home office was the best choice.

Josh was also beginning to work with Chera to produce the *Miners' Directory*.

I didn't really have a say in any of this. I was busy working closely with Kim and doing my job day-to-day in Dawson.

I didn't want any part of Whitehorse. I didn't want any part of the *Miners' Directory*. I just wanted the Insider. It was my baby. I didn't want to see it fail with the first snowfall.

D walked into Jay's trailer one Sunday afternoon. We both had the day off. I think our first conversation was about the macaroni-crunching girl, who had now left.

D worked as the head baker/cook for a new restaurant and retail gold outlet in town. Her hours were long. She was up most days before five a.m. to bake fresh goodies and returned from her cooking duties twelve hours later. I worked most nights. I rarely saw her. I saw her dog, Django, far more.

We were both wondering about our winter plans. Her trailer in the front yard was certainly not going to house her through the next seven months of freezing temperatures.

Her summer job at the café would end soon. She had no idea where she was going to spend the winter. We had a few short weeks before we had to find a new home. Neither of us were making much money.

We had a lot in common.

I loved her dog, which she had picked up as a puppy from an outfitter in the mountains a few miles outside of Whitehorse.

Django once took on an entire sled dog team after its alpha caught wind of her and dragged the entire pack across the frozen Yukon River for a fight. The team was attached to each other and the sled. The driver had no control. The alpha dog was harnessed in the middle of the team. It didn't matter. That dog smelled Django from far away. Both were itching for a fight.

Django versus the team. What a mess. It was a draw. I watched it happen.

Django came out of the skirmish punctured and wounded but with her tail wagging. She finally found a fair fight. She was so pleased with herself.

I had learned to approach Django warily, offering her kindness and respect. She loved most adult humans. She loved food. She loved back scratches. She loved to fight.

Django hated everything else.

No one ever petted her except Jay and I, and I'm not so sure about Jay. Protect your children and pets when Django was around.

Even Aedes Scheer made sure she was in full armour when she came to pinch Django's glands every few months.

D and I both had Sundays off, and we started to spend an hour or two walking Django along Peter's dyke. D was great company.

I remember our first date. We went out to Ruby's, an extremely short-lived attempt at a restaurant in the Callison subdivision, just outside of town.

The restaurant was run by twin sisters. They were Thelma and Selma Bouvier from the *Simpsons* personified. They were big women with big hair. They wore matching dresses, not in colour, but in spirit. They smoked relentlessly, resulting in raspy voices. They were in their late fifties, maybe. We called them The Rubies.

They said they were award-winning cooks. The Rubies wanted to trade advertising for a food credit. I thought I'd take D out there to try it before I made the deal. We chose one of our Sunday afternoons.

The first thing we noticed was the smell of dog crap wafting up from under our table. The second thing we noticed was the mould on the buns that they offered up. Oh man, that meal was a stomach turner.

I remember D and I laughing an awful lot at that meal. She wasn't offended. Neither was I. We ran the Ruby's restaurant ads for months after that. Come for the experience, I thought.

I left for a week to attend my ten-year high school reunion in Calgary. I drove the long trip in the aging, rusty, beat-up Mazda. It made the drive, no problems.

D found a book from the dump, a place she loved to frequent in her ongoing search for lost Klondike treasures: *How to Prepare for Your High School Reunion*. It was from the late 1970s.

She gave it to me before I left. I read every word in preparation. I loved it.

I covered the cost of traveling to Calgary by selling advertising along the Alaska Highway to help build the annual magazine Zig had been creating since 1994.

I figured I should do what I could to build the business. I didn't care much about me. I slept in the truck to save money.

I don't need to go to the big blue bin of newspapers to remind me of what happened next.

I remember returning to Dawson in late September. I had no money to rent a place for the winter. I had nothing to put into a place even if I did find one. The business was about to take on a huge expansion. There was no re-negotiating my low salary. I was stuck.

By October 1, I was sleeping on Zig's couch, homeless again. The unravelling had begun.

Chapter 14
A Season of Growth

I've tried to forget October 1997. Living on a couch in a crowded, beat-up mobile home with winter arriving in the central Yukon is not worthy of the memories.

I know the office was only twenty feet away. I remember I would wake up, walk over to the computer and start work. I would stay there until the couch was free later that night. I never went into the kitchen. I'm not sure if I was allowed to use the shower or not.

It was a terrible existence. My abandoned camper was more comfortable, though it was frozen solid by mid-October.

I have no idea how or where I ate, showered or did laundry. I don't even know where I stored my pack, which contained all that I owned.

My saving grace was work. Work is always the answer.

We were busy. The plan was working. Let's dig through the big blue bin and return to the newspapers of October through December 1997 and see how this tale unfolds.

The story is in the details.

As I peruse the headlines and the weekly table of contents section, which summarizes the staff members and their changing roles, the memories come back slowly.

Each week, the Insider shows how the business was changing.

Josh was selling advertising in Whitehorse. Those ads were being supported by Wills, who was writing about current events in the Yukon's capital city.

I see the first Whitehorse-based ad pop up in the Insider on October 7. They became more regular with each week. Josh was doing his job.

I know that I rented a bedroom in a house in Dawson City for November 1, thanks to an advance from Zig. I didn't want to stay on his couch anymore. A month was enough.

I also see that the Insider continued to grow. By December 1, the paper had jumped in size by fifty percent, from sixteen to twenty-four pages.

The Insider held as much advertising from Whitehorse as it did from Dawson. Josh would sell an ad then collect the information from a client and email it to Chera back at the Klassic, who would design it.

Chera would then fax the draft design back to Whitehorse where Josh would pick it up and show the client.

Changes or approvals would be made following the same process. They repeated this every day for months. The money was rolling in.

This was the first time a Dawson-based newspaper had ever expanded into Whitehorse. Yukon had one hundred years of newspaper history by this time. We were unique.

Sure, the *Klondike Sun* had published advertisements from Whitehorse in its pages for years. But they had never attempted an expansion to Whitehorse. No one had. Advertising space in the *Sun* was booked by publicity agencies in Whitehorse. These ads were few and far between. Whitehorse doesn't think about Dawson City, except when they want to head north for a weekend of partying.

We were different. We were using modern technology and people to change the system. We were drawing money from Whitehorse to support Dawson City. It was a big deal.

If the ad needed a picture, Josh would take it with our second (and better) Olympus digital camera and email it to Chera.

JPEG files were so large in those days, compared to what could be reasonably transferred via internet, that we would use Stuffit to shrink down the photos before emailing them.

Stuffit Expander was used at the other end to open the file and return it to its normal size. We learned to use an FTP site and Fetch software to transfer the files more efficiently. We thought that was pretty clever. We learned there was an internet outside of HTTP. Using

FTP was like traveling on a quiet, secondary highway most people didn't know about.

More importantly, we were starting to put a major dent in the *Klondike Sun's* operations. We were literally starting to kill off our competition.

I thought it was a good thing at the time. That's what newspapers were supposed to do to each other.

Joe Urie had begun to write for us. Joe was still managing the Westminster Hotel. He saw how the Insider was picked up and read regularly in his bar. The Westminster continued to advertise each week. The summer advertising campaign had been a roaring success. The bar was always full, and I often saw patrons flipping through the Insider as they enjoyed a drink and a smoke in the dingy bar.

But winter was arriving, and Joe had to change his marketing plans with the change of season. Joe wanted to attract the hockey crowd to The Pit. Selling post-game beers after local hockey games to the competing players and their friends four nights a week was worth a fortune.

The competition for this beer money was fierce among the three bars that remained open through the winter: The Pit, the Downtown and the Eldorado Hotel.

Joe wanted the money, and he was prepared to work for it. He took his efforts with the Insider well beyond advertising. Joe became a sportswriter.

He invented a character named Ron Cherry that would write a weekly column for the Insider.

I hated it.

No, I didn't hate hockey commentary. I loved local hockey. I loved that hockey players drank beer. I loved that hotels advertise the fact that they loved beer-drinking hockey players as much as I did.

In fact, it was a giant hockey love-in all around.

I simply hated the name Joe chose.

Ron Cherry? As in a cross between Ron Maclean and Don Cherry, the legendary duo that helped us understand what's happening every Saturday on Hockey Night in Canada for more than twenty years?

People would think Joe was arrogant. People would think it was stupid. It wouldn't work.

Zig agreed with me. We even changed Ron's name to Doug Nugget one week without consulting Joe. Zig and I laughed at that name for a while.

Joe didn't.

He was mad. He said we were cracked. He had us change it back. He said hockey players like what they can relate to, and that they can relate to Ron and Don. They couldn't relate to Doug Nugget.

Joe knew his audience way better than we did.

I listened. I believed him. I was wrong. I made the change back. That's what editors sometimes do.

Joe nailed it. Hockey players flocked to The Pit. Joe helped run the league that year. His enthusiasm was infectious.

Players scored goals and the beer flowed. Cheques were signed, bank accounts grew, and tips were earned. It was good times.

Zig was on the road a lot, selling advertising for his annual. I was with him, sometimes, shuffling between Whitehorse and Dawson City.

I remember flat tires. I remember learning how to roll a cigarette while I was at the wheel, long before cell phones and distracted driving tickets were a thing. I remember lots of success, laughter, stress and work.

We were growing fast, learning and having a pretty good time. I didn't really need a home that November. I just lived on the road.

I do remember Kim and Chera starting work each morning next to the woodstove in the Klassic, getting warm, drinking coffee, chatting and rolling enough cigarettes to get them through the day.

I enjoyed those moments a lot when I was around. Kim and Chera were my friends.

Meanwhile, Zig and Josh were establishing the business in Whitehorse.

They had rented a three-bedroom half-duplex in Takhini North to house our growing operations.

This neighbourhood was a run-down former army barracks that housed troops stationed in Whitehorse in the late 1940s and 1950s. The troops were in town to build the Alaska Highway and the Whitehorse airport.

The duplexes were turned over to the Canadian government after the projects were completed and the army went home.

Takhini North had been welfare housing for decades. The neighbourhood contained all the elements of a ghetto. It was beat-up, rough, and transient. The drug trade was rampant.

Cops patrolled daily. The standard army issue rental housing was dilapidated. Nobody cared about the yards.

Piles of trash and discarded household items were everywhere. Dogs were always barking.

It was a true hellhole, but it was cheap for Yukon standards, — about seven hundred-and-fifty dollars a month for rent. We never talked to anyone in the 'hood.

The plan was for me to move to Whitehorse to become the editor of the *Horse's Mouth,* the city's weekly entertainment and TV guide.

Staff would live in the upper two floors. I would get one of the three bedrooms. Josh would get the second one. Zig would occupy the third whenever he was in town. If he wasn't around, the room was up for grabs. Somebody always slept there. We didn't always know who.

I think we bought a couch, a dining room table and a kitchen table from a garage sale. That's all the furniture we had. There were no beds. I would sleep on the floor.

The spacious basement was going to be turned into a publishing office. It had almost no natural light. It was cold and uncomfortable.

By November 25, Kim was editor of the Insider. I would have to work with her remotely by internet, phone and fax from Whitehorse.

I wasn't excited about the move. I wasn't excited about Whitehorse. My negative opinion was created that first morning in 1994, when I bused into the Yukon. I loved my role in Dawson City, and I loved the community. I really liked working with Kim and Chera. We were successful together.

But I also saw that the business model was working. Money was rolling in thanks to pre-Christmas advertising,

I could see that a weekly entertainment magazine was possible. I was on board with the move to Whitehorse. I was on board with growth. Whitehorse was the future.

Zig and I spent most of our time those autumn months building the 1998 annual, which I won't name in order to respect his wishes. It was a very successful publication. It still is.

Zig had been publishing the annual since 1994. He built the first issues in the *Klondike Sun* office, where he traded volunteer time for space on their computers, layout tables and publishing equipment.

By 1997, Zig had created a magazine with over one hundred-thousand dollars in advertising revenue.

Zig came up with the idea while he was spending the winter surviving in a wall tent in the Klondike valley with temperatures that regularly dropped to minus thirty Celsius and lower.

His annual covered stories, business and attractions on all the highways from Dawson Creek, BC (mile zero on the Alaska Highway); to Inuvik, NWT; to Tok, Alaska; to Beaver Creek, Yukon; and south along the Stewart Cassiar Highway into central BC. It was a vast area covering thousands of square kilometres.

Zig seemed to know every advertiser in this region personally. He found writers wherever he went. He always has. We are a dime a dozen. So are advertisers. Zig had been driving the various northern routes for years. He loved it.

Zig's favorite story was figuring out what to do with one hundred-thousand annuals when they were dumped by a huge truck on his front step at the Klassic one April morning in 1997. They filled his entire yard.

I think flags are waved and banners are raised when Zig arrives in Tok, Alaska, to sell ads each summer.

They love him there.

Americans appreciate advertising opportunities far more than Canadians. They are simply more aggressive when it comes to business. Zig thrives in America.

Besides editing the Insider, my job was to gather text and fill the growing annual with stories. I learned quickly how to make a lot more money by doing this. I discovered the beauty of the advertorial before that term even existed. I would pick successful, interesting business in our area and ask if they wanted a full-page story written about them.

I could guarantee one hundred-thousand copies the following year and distribution in the vast area. I guaranteed they had the right to final edit. I charged one thousand two hundred dollars for my service. I think I sold a dozen that fall. It was a high paying cold call. Zig was ecstatic. I later heard that one business made a thirty-five-thousand dollar sale on hand-crafted Klondike gold jewelry off the story that I wrote.

Everything was clicking. I could see how being in Whitehorse could be a good step for my financial future. I was buying into the move.

Dawson was the end of the road; Whitehorse was the centre. There were a lot more advertorials to write in the capitol. There were a lot more ads to sell. There was simply a lot more money to earn. Or so we all believed.

Zig was on fire about Whitehorse. I'd never seen him so excited. Growth could be his middle name. He is never still. Zig is either growing or shrinking.

He had even expanded into tiny Atlin, BC, and had found McNutt, who would sell ads for the annual and let us run his cartoon, *Melonhead*, in our papers.

As I dig deeper into my big blue bin the memories surface.

I remember being in Inuvik, near the Arctic Ocean, selling advertising that autumn, enjoying the incredible colours of the deserted Dempster Highway as I drove.

Every Canadian should experience this highway in early September. The fall colours are spectacular, and the road is empty. Inuvik in September should be on any globetrotter's checklist.

I also remember driving more than one thousand three hundred kilometres south to Atlin, in the same week, to meet McNutt. Distances between communities in northern Canada can be phenomenal.

But I mostly remember the countless hours discussing the equipment, cash and logistics we needed to pull off this expansion.

Starting a weekly entertainment magazine in a city we barely knew was no small task. We needed tables and chairs. We needed computers. We needed a scanner, a fax machine, another tabloid laser printer. We needed office supplies. We needed another graphic artist. We needed writers. We needed a photographer.

We needed to connect everything so it could be shared flawlessly back at Dawson City headquarters. We needed food. We needed toilet paper. We needed a lot.

I was worried about the cash burn rate. We were spending money earmarked to print the annual in April on the start-up of the *Horse's Mouth*. It was a big risk. I knew it would take time to make the money back.

Zig wasn't worried. As long as he had space on his credit card, everything would be fine. He never looked past his available credit. He had no problems operating in debt. I did. I hated debt and we were about to fall very deeply into it.

Chapter 15
Outside and Back

D was back!

I was bouncing all over the north in the fall of 1997 and had forgotten about her.

While away, she realized that the Klondike was her best home option. She didn't know where else to go. She sold off her few belongings and headed back north, just in time for winter.

I had rented a room in a house and the owner, Tim, was taking off for a few months. He had another available bedroom and wanted someone to cover the mortgage while he was gone. I told D about the place. She jumped at it.

Finding a home in Dawson City is always tough. I suddenly had a new roomie. I still had Django for protection.

But with my move to Whitehorse imminent, I didn't think too much about my living quarters nor my roomie.

I was on the way out of Dawson City before Christmas, and until I left, I had a mountain of work and a lot of travel to keep me busy.

When Kim, Zig, Chera and I were all in the office, we were short a computer. We only had three.

The office was busy and a difficult place to write. The phone never stopped ringing, people never stopped coming by, cramping the tiny space.

I used to unplug a computer at night, bring it home from the office and write by the warm fire.

I was happy at Tim's place. I was a Klondike writer building a business and penning the stories I wanted. I stoked the woodstove and worked in silence.

I would return the computer to the office each morning. Somehow, the four of us bounced between the computers and still managed to meet all of our deadlines.

Advertising for the *Miner's Directory* was selling, the annual was selling, the Insider was selling. We were making a killing.

As much as I enjoy journalism, it was the money that attracted me to the publishing business. Journalism was never going to be about money, that's still true. But publishing? It's like printing money.

And the money was there. Each time Zig or I would go to the mailbox, it was full of cheques. They could range from forty to two thousand dollars. We would often sit and open them together — stacks of them at a time.

It was great. It was better than anything I'd experienced in my short career. We both loved making money and we knew our costs. The margins were amazing.

We described the stories in the paper among ourselves as "the shit between the ads".

I still explain to people that ads are placed in a newspaper template first, then the writing is used to fill in the space around the ads.

The more ads we had, the less money and time we had to spend on writing. This money-making formula was countered by the cost of the number of pages printed to balance the writing and the ads. We still had to attract readers with content so that the ads worked for the advertisers. It was a constant balancing act to keep the Insider profitable yet readable; more ads meant more pages meant more text required to fill the holes.

The catch is that publications don't jump in size by just one page. They must jump by a multiple of four pages. It's just the way the printing process works.

Growing the sixteen-page Insider therefore meant a minimum twenty-five percent increase in size.

This large growth required selling at least twenty-five percent more ads and writing twenty-five percent more text, which meant more work and expense. This effort was hopefully balanced by far more than a twenty-five percent increase in profit. That's the point of growth.

It's a big deal to find, write and publish four more pages of stories in the same time period. It's difficult but I loved this balancing act. I still do. I wish the watered-down internet hadn't killed the power of profitability in the print world, which is now a shadow of its former self.

Zig didn't care if there were any stories at all. He rarely read them anyway. He didn't care about balance like I did.

The phone in the Klassic was relentless. People were coming and going daily. The office was never quiet.

We were now building four publications and prepping for a fifth: the annual, the annual translated into German, the Insider, the *Miner's Directory* and the *Horse's Mouth*.

All the publications were growing. Deadlines were being met but the workload was getting out of control far too quickly.

We were also managing the desktop publishing work that continued to flow in. We even made a killing off our manual laminating machine.

We would print off a page, stick it in a plastic sleeve, then run it through this tiny electric machine, which heated up the acetate enough to melt it to the paper by running it through two rubber rollers.

We charged three dollars for a twenty-cent sleeve. We had the only commercial laminator in town. Almost every poster or menu designed in Dawson City was run through our laminator.

Each sleeve took about a minute to run through the machine. It was an amazing mark up. Nothing has ever made money for me as effectively as our laminating machine.

Managing this workload was an enormous task for five people, but each day, we grew a little stronger.

To match the growth, we needed to contract freelancers. We maxed out at twenty people on the team by mid-January. We grew from two to twenty people in just eight months.

Josh was talking up the *Horse's Mouth* in Whitehorse. People were interested. Advertisers said they were committing. We were on our way.

Back in Dawson, D was off duty for a few months. She needed the break. We spent a lot of time talking, laughing, enjoying each other's company at Tim's place.

Maybe it was because I liked her dog. Maybe it was the northern lights. Maybe it was just us. Sparks eventually lit. Still, I had committed to Whitehorse and I was going to stick to my guns. By the first week of December, I was in Whitehorse. The romantic house on the hill was behind me.

Joe Urie came to town one night before Christmas and we went out for drinks with a few friends.

Our friend Renee was there. She brought her friend Julie. They were originally from Quebec and had gone to school together. I knew Renee but not Julie.

We had fun that night. We were drinking eight-dollar pitchers of draft in some 1970s-era bar that has long since been flattened and replaced by riverfront condominiums.

The joke was on Renee. She was drunk enough that she failed to notice each time somebody slipped some change into her glass.

Loonies, quarters, and dimes were dropped in her beer mug. She would sip, someone would refill her glass. Someone else would slip in a nickel. By the end of the night, she had more money than beer in her glass. She never noticed. I'm not sure who kept the money. We probably spent it on another round at last call.

I talked to Julie that night. I told her about my imminent move to Whitehorse. She was living about ten kilometres out of Dawson City and she didn't have a vehicle. It was her first winter in the Klondike and she was feeling isolated. Julie wanted to move into town. We agreed that she could rent my bedroom and live with D. It was settled. I was truly on my way again. I had barely moved in.

I flew back to my childhood home in Calgary for Christmas that year. In those days, it was cheaper to drive than fly.

Gas was around sixty cents a litre in Whitehorse. We could get about six hundred kilometres out of a forty-litre gas tank, so it took about five tanks of gas to drive from Whitehorse to Calgary — a cost of about one hundred and twenty dollars.

In contrast, the Air Canada flight was about one thousand two hundred dollars, and it wasn't direct. I had to fly to Vancouver first, then Calgary. I always drove in those early years. It was way too expensive to fly.

This has all changed. Whitehorse-based Air North started flying south in 2000. Air North had been in business flying around the north for decades. The company saw an opportunity for expansion and took it after attracting a major investor — The Vuntut Gwich'in First Nation out of Old Crow, Yukon. The VGFN had also just settled its land claim with the federal government and negotiated to invest in Air North with the massive pay-out.

This investment paved the way for Air North to begin flights from Whitehorse to Vancouver, then Edmonton and Calgary. Air North has been doing so ever since. It changed the way Yukon relates with the world dramatically.

Now, a flight on Air North from Whitehorse to Calgary can be bought round trip for about five hundred dollars. This is less than half of the cost on Air Canada in 1998.

People rarely drive now, as the cost of gas has doubled. Air North flights are always full.

Christmas in Calgary was insignificant. I saw my parents, my siblings and my old friends.

I was ready to leave again after a couple of days. The rest was good for me, but I was excited about the new opportunities that were waiting in Whitehorse. I was about to start up a new entertainment magazine and

I believed there was plenty of advertising money to support it.

My enthusiasm bubbled over. My old friend JP from journalism school was also in Calgary. He had specialized in photography and was looking for work.

I told him we might be able to use someone to help sell ads, take photos and generally help out. He was in. He was prepared to drive north to Whitehorse on New Year's Eve. I contacted Zig. He said to bring JP along. He knew we needed the help.

I was back in Whitehorse by December 28. The turkey had hardly digested. I was ready to begin work on our first issue of the *Horse's Mouth*.

JP began his drive to Whitehorse as he said he would, on December 31, 1997. His journey ended later that night, in Dawson Creek, BC.

His car failed just eight hours into the trip. He was still twenty hours away from Whitehorse, completely stuck.

The car would take a week to fix because no mechanics were available. JP had very little money – certainly not enough to repair the car and drive to Whitehorse nor wait around in an expensive hotel to get it fixed.

Zig didn't go anywhere that Christmas. He stayed in Dawson City and worked away. He found Paulette, a graphic artist in Whitehorse, who was looking for part-time work. She was perfect for the *Horse's Mouth*.

Paulette lived in a house with Doogie, who did very little. Doogie loved to roll and smoke, roll and smoke, break for coffee, then roll and smoke. That's all he ever did.

When JP failed to show, we had to come up with a plan. We felt responsible for him. We couldn't just abandon him in Dawson Creek.

We told JP to leave his car in Dawson Creek until a mechanic could fix it and get on the Greyhound bus to Whitehorse.

At our end, we put Doogie on the bus and sent him south to Dawson Creek a few days behind JP. We filled his tobacco pouch and gave him a few bucks for food.

Doogie bused down to Dawson Creek, picked up the car and drove it to Whitehorse where it was reunited with JP.

It cost us an insane amount of money. Doogies don't come cheap. Neither do JPs.

When Zig first met JP, all he could think about was how much he had already cost him. It was not a good start.

Chapter 16
The Horse's Mouth

The Whitehorse TV guide was a mess.

We were offering the new expanded listings as part of our entertainment magazine and we couldn't figure it out.

Unfortunately, neither could WHTV, the local television service provider.

Steve Robertson was dumping the guide on us, and Zig believed we could make a profit.

How we could succeed at this when the venerable *Yukon News* didn't, well, that was never discussed.

The first issue of the *Horse's Mouth* was scheduled for January 15, 1998.

Could we pick a more difficult date to begin a business in the Yukon?

Outside of our ghetto duplex, it was minus forty Celsius. Nobody was going out. Nobody could possibly need their TV guide enough to venture outdoors even far enough to plug in their vehicles.

And certainly, nobody was advertising right after Christmas.

It was probably the dumbest possible date to start a publication. January is not December when it comes to the world of advertising. That revenue stream dries up after New Year's Day for every publication operating in the Christian world. All money spent to drive sales in December is carefully guarded in January, to begin the annual cycle anew. Trying to talk advertisers into spending their limited cash in January is no easy sell anywhere.

Steve Robertson knew about January sales, and he was happy to unload the TV guide on us during Yukon's coldest days of the year.

It wasn't my job to sell ads, organize television listings, or manage print runs. Those responsibilities were up to Josh and Zig.

I was working to fill thirty-two pages of content in time for the first edition — eight pages more than the largest ad-filled Insider I'd created before Christmas.

We had another problem, too.

The *Miner's Directory* deadline had arrived. Chera and Josh had been working on it for months. They had met their advertising quota, but much of the layout work still had to be done.

The whole thing had to be completed and printed in January — just days before we were scheduled to publish the first *Horse's Mouth*.

Josh and Zig had to work on the *Miner's Directory*, so they weren't working the streets selling *Horse's Mouth* advertising.

JP had come to be a photographer. He was never going to sell an ad.

I had ignored the *Miners' Directory* project from the start like a bad illness. Now I had to pitch in.

For some reason, we had to type in about four hundred postal codes the night before we could send it to press. I have no idea why this was required, but the client requested it, so we did it.

D was heading to Mexico from Dawson City in early January to celebrate her birthday and get out of the cold. She spent the night at the *Horse's Mouth* house. She came to see me.

We put her to work.

Read me every one of these postal codes, one at a time, as I type them into the computer, I told her.

She looked at me like I was nuts. Then she agreed. D was always up for a challenge.

We were up all night, reading and typing: Y1A 2S9. Got it? Got it. Y1A 3S9. Ok? Ok. Y1A 4T7. Got it? On it went, hour after hour. Who ever said publishing was always sexy?

The work was terrible and lasted all night. At least she got to go to Mexico the next morning.

D and I would smoke a little, then type some more. Everyone was working on something in the cold, dark, smoky basement of the *Horse's Mouth* in January 1998.

What a hellhole. The unfinished basement was concrete with no interior walls, just a large concrete foundation, a concrete floor, a giant oil burning furnace and an indoor heating oil tank that was filled from above ground, outside.

There was one naked light bulb hanging from the unfinished ceiling.

The glow of our three or four computer monitors lit up the underground dim.

We had purchased cheap hollow doors to use as tabletops. We ran them side by side, short end to short end, along the walls to build rudimentary tables.

We used boxes of paper as legs to keep the tables off the ground.

Every table had an ashtray.

We set our computers on the tables then figured out how to ethernet them all together.

Does anyone remember this concept? Ethernet. Funny.

It was the system Apple used back in the day to daisy chain our multiple Macintosh computers together so they could coordinate with each other.

This is long before wireless internet was invented.

The point was to share files to one central serving computer from all the other computers. This was essential to make sure all the files were accurately stored in one accessible folder.

This is standard practice in publishing to ensure the most up-to-date ad, photo or story is published.

There were two types of cords back then.

There was the standard telephone line that inserted into the back of the computer and then into the telephone outlet in the wall. That got us onto the internet.

Then there was the ethernet cord that looked almost identical to the telephone cord, except the toggle that clicked into the back of the computer was a little bigger.

We were constantly changing the cords to move between the internet and the ethernet because the systems would not work simultaneously. We either used the ethernet or the internet, not both.

Ridiculous.

When we needed to share files with the Dawson office, we used the internet. When we needed to share between computers in Whitehorse only, we switched to the ethernet.

The system worked, but my goodness it was cumbersome.

It was also prone to errors. Sometimes, when an ethernet cord was unplugged, then re-plugged, the connection to the central computer would disappear.

We would have to reboot the computers to re-establish the connection through the ethernet software.

It was frustrating and time consuming. Computers rebooted slowly back then. File sharing had yet to be perfected and none of us were trained technicians.

We figured it out on the fly.

Cash was becoming a concern. We spent a lot of money to get set up. How much? I'd have to say close to ten thousand dollars off the top to purchase more computer equipment, rent a place, keep a couple of vehicles on the road, pay freelance writers, and fill the giant oil tank to keep us from freezing alive.

We had to pay for Doogie's bus ticket. We had to pay for JP's bus ticket. We had to pay Kim and Chera to keep the Dawson office going. We had to eat. We had a lot of bills.

Unfortunately, I wasn't one of those bills. I had foregone my one hundred dollar a week salary and wasn't getting paid at all. I'm not sure if anyone in Whitehorse was.

The first edition of the *Horse's Mouth* came out on time, January 15, 1998. We decided to charge one dollar for it, just like the *Yukon News*.

I now go deep into my big blue bin and find that first issue. It's buried under all the Insiders. I rarely dig it out. I count up the ads and shake my head. Eight. That's right. Eight. In a thirty-two-page newspaper. Painful. In comparison, the profitable Insider would have published eight ads in just two pages.

I tried not to make advertising my concern. My job was to fill the magazine with content, not advertising.

Still, I was worried. The numbers didn't lie. We were in trouble. Compared to the immediate success of the Insider, we were publishing a loser.

We spent all night finishing that first edition. With so few ads, we had giant holes to fill. We all worked hard. We all came through. We had coming events, reviews, features on fashion, culture, radio, sports, movies and TV. We even had a local horoscope writer.

And, of course, we had those all-so-important TV guide listings.

JP was the staff photographer and didn't like the quality of our digital camera. Dean was one of the first *Horse's Mouth* writers. He agreed with JP. Dean donated his outdated darkroom equipment to the cause.

JP shot film with his own camera and set up a darkroom in the bathroom. The prints turned out great but time consuming and the film and chemicals were expensive. The only bathroom in our home office seemed to always be occupied by an enlarger, processing chemicals and JP.

He traded an ad with a Whitehorse camera store to cover the cost of the film, chemicals and printing paper. I know they billed us anyway. It wasn't much of a trade.

I held my pee a lot and just let JP do his thing as the prints did look great. He was right. The quality of the film photos scanned into the computer then printed off the laser printer was outstanding — far greater than our point-and-shoot digital camera of 1997 could offer.

But in the end, the quality of his expensive prints didn't really matter.

Most of the detail in JP's black and white prints was lost when transferred to the world of newspaper, where prints always turn grey.

Zig knew this going in. He hated the darkroom/bathroom experiment. It was a waste of time, space and money to him. He wasn't wrong. JP was expensive.

We had stories and photos and columnists, but most importantly, we had that TV guide to try and sell advertising around.

Sadly, and critically, the TV guide didn't work.

Oh, the *Horse's Mouth* looked great and offered lots for a dollar, but the TV guide itself was a mess.

WHTV was going through a significant change to offer expanded cable packages.

To do this, they had to change all the current channel numbers. The changeover wasn't going so well and the information that was provided to us wasn't timely. The channel numbers we published were all wrong.

The TV guide was wrong! What the hell?

What the guide said was on Channel 35 may have been on Channel 79. I didn't realize it was possible to screw up a TV guide. I learned that it was.

On top of this, WHTV went on strike just as we were about to publish. The technicians refused to work, so the channel problem wasn't getting fixed any time soon. Nobody was even in the office to talk to us.

How do you sell advertising around a TV guide that didn't work? How do you sell a TV guide for a dollar when the listings were all wrong?

We didn't know there was a problem until after the first issue came out. No one ever turned on a television at the office to check – we didn't have a TV. Who doesn't trust a TV guide?

The telephone started ringing soon after the paper was in the stores.

I thought nobody was using the TV guide. I was wrong. People were mad.

They wanted the *Yukon News*. They didn't want to buy another paper, costing them another dollar.

They also wanted the TV guide to be accurate.

They certainly didn't want to change their TV habits on January 15. They wanted what they knew.

It wasn't our fault, we tried to explain, but how do you explain that? Our excuses didn't matter. We published it. We were the *Horse's Mouth*.

I remember we worked all night to finish that first edition. We then went to the '98 Hotel Breakfast Club for shots and beers at about nine a.m.

We were all completely exhausted. We had given everything we had to get it off the ground.

It was the hardest way I'd ever lost money in my life. It was the exact opposite of the laminating machine, which made us a relative fortune with no effort at all. We should have simply opened a laminating business in Whitehorse.

Two weeks in and I was already burning out.

Fortunately, fatigue can easily be overcome in the short term by adding on more stress. Adrenaline takes over. I needed that rush, and it came. There was a much bigger concern than outdated TV listings that I was soon to learn about.

As publisher, Zig decided how many copies of everything were to be printed.

Each week, every copy of the Insider was distributed and picked up. The public was happy, and the advertisers were happy. It was a good formula, summer, fall and winter.

That's how it was supposed to work; no extra costs, no extra papers — get them out the door, gone. Make people look for it.

Zig and Steve had negotiated a print run of five thousand copies of the first *Horse's Mouth*. I remember the number clearly, now more than twenty years later.

That's right, five thousand magazines printed for a town of about twenty thousand people.

That meant that one out of every four people in Whitehorse would need to spend a dollar each to clear out all our stock.

And the TV guide, which didn't work anyway, only had those eight advertisements to support the publishing costs.

When the bundles of magazines came off the press, I saw that they kept coming and coming. I questioned Zig about the numbers.

He wanted to blanket Whitehorse. He wanted everyone to know we were the new magazine in town. He expected to sell them all.

I sunk.

Five thousand? What the hell? I cared a lot about losing money unnecessarily.

Why don't we print just a few hundred and make people look for it? I asked Zig.

I remember he raised his eyebrows and rubbed his head. He had not considered this. He had never thought about even talking to me about it.

Steve wanted the presses to roll and he didn't want the heat for removing the TV guide from the *Yukon News* after decades of printing it. He wanted people to buy the *Horse's Mouth*. He wanted us to succeed and cut his costs.

He wanted Zig to handle all of it while he made money on the printing, of course.

Zig had taken the bait: hook, line and sinker.

I think we sold less than one hundred copies of our first edition of the *Horse's Mouth*. We had about four thousand nine hundred extra unsold copies to deal with. We stacked them in our large basement. We didn't even have a woodstove to burn them in.

Just three weeks into my move to Whitehorse, I had a bad feeling that we were not going to last.

I had no time to worry about it.

Dawson was calling. It was time to publish the Insider.

Kim and Chera had their own troubles.

The Klassic had frozen solid. The temperature was dipping to around minus fifty in Dawson and the little trailer couldn't keep up.

The furnace was working, but it couldn't provide enough heat to keep the office warm.

Some days, Kim and Chera typed with mittens on to avoid frostbite in the office.

The trailer cracked and twisted as the thin, metal membrane expanded and shrank with the dramatic temperature difference between the outside cold and the inside warmth.

Power was spotty. So was the furnace. The internet was even spottier. Frozen water lines were an ongoing issue. The woodstove kept the office from icing over completely.

The girls were often more concerned with surviving than with publishing. They had to be. That's life in the Klondike in January. Somehow, they managed to do both.

There was little news to be found in Dawson City that month. Advertising had dried up as predicted. They were stumped as to how to fill the pages.

So, I helped from Whitehorse.

I would unplug the ethernet cord and plug in the phone cord, then dial the internet, connect and hope that the phone lines connecting Dawson to Whitehorse had not snapped in the cold.

This connection happened almost every day.

Kim would also connect in Dawson: plug in, dial up, connect and hope we would stay connected.

We would share most of the text, photos and ads over the phone lines necessary to fill the many empty spaces in our publications over the phone lines.

Some completed pages were also shipped back and forth on Air North because the files were too big to be sent over the internet.

I would help layout pages in Whitehorse. Kim would do the same in Dawson City. Then she would transfer her files to Whitehorse where I'd combine them with the *Horse's Mouth* to complete the Insider.

We would inexplicably disconnect all the time.

I would connect through a local Whitehorse internet service provider; she would do the same through Dawson.

But there was a hitch.

Sometimes, the ISP in Dawson was down. Ravens, cold, lack of staff, multiple users, whatever, would cause a disconnect during the middle of a file transfer or prevent connection altogether.

With no other choice and deadlines looming, Kim would sometimes use the Whitehorse ISP to connect to the internet out of Dawson. It was more reliable.

This was a local Whitehorse number but a long-distance number in Dawson.

Therefore, we would be charged a long-distance rate, by the minute, when she logged onto the internet through the Whitehorse number.

Kim would go back and forth between the two ISP phone numbers daily, trying to get online, move files, meet deadlines, fill the paper and not spend extra money. She did it all at minus fifty. She was amazing.

Back in Whitehorse, Zig wasn't overly worried about our early troubles.

He had an ace-in-the-hole to cover the loss. He was heading to Arizona that month to sell his annual. Zig and McNutt, from Atlin, had hatched another plan that couldn't fail. They were going to the world's largest recreational vehicle gathering in Quartsite, Arizona, to peddle the annual for a dollar.

Zig had used this trip as a carrot to lure advertisers to the annual in the fall sales season. He promised distribution in Arizona in January. It was a credible sales device.

Back then, RV drivers flocked to Dawson City. Tens of thousands of them drove the Alaska and Klondike highways each summer. Thousands of those RV owners also ended up in Quartsite every winter to bask in the warm, southern sun before moving on in the beginning of spring.

This transient townsite in the desert supported a huge RV trade show – one of the world's largest. It was like Burning Man for retired Americans. Zig was confident he could sell the annual to the thousands of folks that showed up over the course of a week or two.

Somebody once told me that all Americans wish to reach two destinations before they die: Las Vegas and Alaska. Yukon was on the way to Alaska. They had to drive right through us. Zig figured they needed his annual to do so.

It was a good promotional pitch to prospective advertisers.

There was a hitch though — the annual wasn't ready for publishing in January. Not even close. It would be months before it was completely finished and ready for Yukon's summer crowd, its traditional audience.

To get around this, Zig laid out a smaller version in the *Horse's Mouth* office and saved it on two zip disks. His plan was to get it printed when he was in Arizona. It sounded reasonable. It turned out it wasn't. Shortly after we churned out our first issue of the *Horse's Mouth*, Zig was on the road.

He and McNutt left town with the temperature still hovering in the minus thirties most of the way south. A couple of hours after crossing the US border, the little Mazda B2200 pick-up truck broke down.

Our remaining cash was about to disappear.

Chapter 17
Klondike Erotic

I still have five issues of the *Horse's Mouth* tucked away in the big blue bin under my sixty-one issues of the Dawson City Insider.

There should be two more, but they've long since disappeared. I have no idea where they went. If you still have one of these few relics of Whitehorse's publishing past, drop me a line. I'd love to complete the set, even if I don't read a word.

I rarely open them today. I simply don't want to. Some memories should be left buried deep in the big blue bin.

Where was I?

Oh yes.

Zig and McNutt had broken down in Montana or Washington State. The fully loaded Mazda B2200 just didn't have the will to climb over all the mountains between Dawson City and Arizona, especially in the coldest part of winter.

These kinds of troubles rarely affected Zig. They still don't.

He's like a weeble. He's had a thousand incidents since then and he's still in business. He never falls down. He's truly remarkable. He'll always just get back in the truck and find a solution.

I remember one time we were selling ads in Alaska.

We spent the night at a country house bed and breakfast. He traded an ad for a couple nights' stay with the owner.

This trade made for free accommodation and a home base to sell more advertising in the area.

On our way out of the driveway, he backed into the host's hand-built, wooden mailbox. It rattled to the ground.

Zig is a stand up-guy. He got out of the same Mazda B2200 and picked up the fallen mailbox.

He knocked on the door and handed it to our unsuspecting host. Zig said sorry, walked to the truck and drove away. The host said nothing. She was speechless. She just stood there holding her mailbox in the doorway.

Did their ad run in the next year's annual? Hard to say. Zig certainly wouldn't remember but he probably found a way to smooth things over without building her a new mailbox.

The truck got fixed in Washington or Montana, Zig lost a couple of days in time, and the bank account was sucked down another few hundred dollars.

No worries, he was on his way. On to Arizona!

Zig had arranged to print that small version of his annual at a printing press near Quartsite.

He had prepared it meticulously back in Whitehorse, spending hours on the computer in the bowels of *The Horse's Mouth*. It looked good onscreen, not great. It was a fraction of its normal size.

Sadly, Zig forgot one of the two zip discs full of files back in Whitehorse, or he lost it on the way when the truck broke down.

He had parts of the annual with him but not all of it.

He had some files on the one disk that he still had packed in the truck. Without access to the internet to get the missing files back from Whitehorse, he had to build the rest of the layout on the road.

Living out of the truck, he cobbled together some sort of a Frankenstein publication at some printing press and got to the Quartsite RV show.

I have no idea how he did it, but that is Zig's story to tell. I wasn't there. These things happen, as Zig always says. Did I mention it was one of the biggest RV shows in the world? Zig wasn't going to let a little thing like missing half the files slow him down from selling.

Kim and Chera were keeping the home fires burning back in Dawson. The Klondike had gone to sleep. People were cozied up to their woodstoves and keeping their eyes on power and water. Society had stopped at fifty below, which is dangerously cold.

Kim decided to experiment with a little creative writing to fill the pages of the Insider. With sparse news, she didn't have many options.

A Girl on My Tongue was introduced when a new writer appeared in town.

Today, Kim and I agree on what *Girl* meant to the history of the Insider.

We both wanted *Girl* published for the same reasons.

The town was dead and buried in snow and cold. Nobody moved.

There were very few advertisers and those businesses that did advertise wouldn't care what we published.

Why not throw a little heat into January to attract attention?

Well let's put it to you, gentle reader. Would you run it?

Here is *There's a Girl on My Tongue* from Jan 27, 1998. It's a beaut.

Her Side: A Midwinter's Tirade

I bestow upon you, my conundrum.
Benign expression.

It was a typically hazardous week. Hazardous because it was not Christmas, nor New Year's, nor fifty below. It was average.

There is nothing more perilous than an average week. Everything about my ever-so-complacent self is luminously spreading out before me.

Okay, girls, there's a ton of us around this town. Vigorous, passionate, intelligent creatures, and we don't always walk softly.

It's time we had a diminutive, weekly utterance.

No offence, guys. Besides, you've got your hockey teams; a comradery I quickly became envious of whilst witnessing your intimate convocation sip and share all secrets during a ceremonial Saturday night social incident.

Although, women, too, hold invaluable insight in our crevices. So please, come along.

Yup, it's the dead of winter and we're thinking about you boys more than we'd like to.

Those of us (girls) who aren't getting giant cuddles (etc.) on a regular schedule, or at all, feeling libido temporarily rise between TV channels and menstrual cycles.

Yes, we are amorous.

And for women, our amorous needs can mean life possessing enslavement to the object, or objects, of our lurid longings.

I read somewhere that men have fantasies every twenty minutes during the day. (Apparently, this slows at night when testosterone levels dip.).

Ok. I think I can read this in *Cosmo* — do your own research. Women, from my experience (which is better than *Cosmo's*) don't get a break from fantasies.

Women live the fantasy. Wake every morning into it… squirm through the banal workday with it… slip into sleepy, dreamy, subconscious with it. It consumes her.

Thought becomes obsessive, lustful, postulation. She sprinkles it on her cereal. She takes it for walks. She drinks it. The oblivion of 'the crush.'

When I was finally released from my horrifying high school, I expected also to be released from 'crushes.' I had my liberation to attend to.

The domination of my heart and spirit by extraneous forces was to end. My estranged self-thrived off the freedom of anonymity.

Ah, fickle youth. To keep this story slight, I bring you back to now… the redolent, updated version of my discontented female.

Usurp this craze.

Voice feminine frenzy and fervour.

How else do we endure sensual suffocation? We don't need the *Bartender* to answer our afflictions — there are no answers.

Share clandestine angst. If you can't find a lover to ease the ravenous gnawing… FOUND A COLUMN! Face Your Fever.

Lovingly,
Girl on My Tongue.

***

With eyebrows raised, I let my vision shift to the next page of that January 27, 1998 Insider, directly across from *Girl*.

It's Potoroka's *Market Report*, which meticulously explores the beauty of menstruation through art in four vibrant columns. It truly should be read to be believed.

Below the *Market Report* sits our friend John Wierda's financial column, buried under art and longing, but true to his word — Mr. Reliable.

Maybe it was just the January blues, maybe staff in Dawson were feeling particularly lonely or just desperate for content, but sex was taking over the Insider.

I know we were not thinking about sex in Whitehorse.

The fridge was empty back at *The Horse's Mouth*.

We had traded an ad for a food credit with Whitehorse's long-gone Blackstone Café, but they closed at lunch, so we had to eat early or not at all.

I don't remember what we did when the food ran out. We probably just smoked more and didn't think about it. There was enough work to keep our brains occupied. Nicotine helped curb our appetites. Food was a hassle.

We were now publishing two issues a week. The *Horse's Mouth* on Thursdays and the Insider on Tuesdays.

As I said, Kim would finish most of the template in Dawson and then 'FTP' it to me in Whitehorse. I would then take the best of the *Horse's Mouth* pages and insert them into the Insider, then I'd take it to the press.

I barely glanced at the stuff Kim sent me. I had too many tasks in Whitehorse. Plus, I trusted her.

Then I saw *There's a Girl on My Tongue* and it stopped me in my tracks.

Really?

I had to think about publishing this. The paper was due at the printer. I had to make a decision. I could easily cut out this column. I could easily cut out the *Market Report*.

But why?

I agreed with Kim. Let's spice things up a bit. I let it run.

There were no complaints from our Dawson readers. There was no lost ad revenue. *Girl* wrote two more. They were brilliant. Again, no complaints. All seemed well.

The Insider was surviving the winter, or so it seemed from Whitehorse.

But shall we hear the story directly from Kim? She lived it.

Here's what she has to say about that intense January in the Klondike, over twenty years ago.

***

The first few months of the Insider were a chaotic blur. The sun never set, and we tried to keep pace. Dawson was a flurry of activity that we chased down each week with notepad and camera, then transformed into content back at the trailer.

I'd like to think that Chris, Zig and I got into a groove, but it was often an awkward two steps forward, one step back kind of rhythm.

As we worked through the challenges on the publishing end, we didn't lack for story material. That would change.

When summer comes rapidly to a close in Dawson, a type of hibernation sets in. Community events wind down, summer workers migrate back south, and more than half of the hotels and restaurants shut down and board up.

Come fall, not only had we lost most of our motley crew of volunteer writers, but there was meagre fodder for stories.

With the "closed for the season" signs going up, we lost a fair chunk of our key advertisers, meaning we had even more blank space to fill.

But with what? Moose meat recipes? Snow shovelling tips? Curling box scores?

Some weeks we had big stories — the Yukon Quest, Trek Over the Top, Thaw-Di-Gras. But some weeks it seemed that nothing was going on. I had to generate stories out of cold thin air.

The content was my responsibility. Zig and Chris were trying to capture the Whitehorse market.

I was at the helm of the Insider.

I wrote my first editorial about what every other editor across the world was reflecting on — the deaths of Mother Theresa and Princess Diana.

I could not for the life of me figure out how the hell any of this affected our frozen little town.

I threw together a few banal sentences at the deadline — so few that I had to increase the font size to fill the editorial space, briefly mortified for doing so, but determined to put that Insider to bed and get on to the next one.

We knew people were reading it. Mostly we knew this because folks love to let you know when you've done something wrong.

About half an hour after the paper hit the shelves each Tuesday, we started getting calls about typos or spelling mistakes. Every week. Without fail. Early on we capitalized on this phenomenon and turned it into a contest.

The first to call with the correct number of typos won a free coffee courtesy of Riverwest. Now we had readers devouring the Insider front to back in quest of a free coffee.

Some readers even believed the mistakes were there on purpose, rather than as a result of bleary-eyed last-minute keystrokes. It was brilliant.

Not only was it the first winter for the Insider, but most of the Insider gang was facing the harsh initiation of a Yukon winter. We were mostly cheechakos.

It was often a struggle to keep both the home and office fires burning, both literally and metaphorically.

One morning, Chera and I arrived at the trailer to find that not only had the insides of the windows and walls iced up, but the computer cords were covered in frost.

And it was dark. The chart of daylight hours we inserted each week into the Insider showed daylight had plummeted from twenty-four hours mid-summer to four in January.

For weeks we did not see the sun at all.

Chera was my personal sunbeam. My Girl Friday. She was my best friend, and my work wife, now that my work husband had left me for the *Horses' Mouth*.

Chera worked on ads and layout, all the while filling the trailer with her goofy laughter.

When I was at my wit's end, staring at a blank spot I had no idea how to fill, I'd often send Chera out into the cold with the digital camera to get a shot of something. Anything.

She was a miracle worker with a good eye. She bundled up and headed out. She always found a shot that worked.

I loved my Insider boys — bringing Wayne on was a stroke of genius. And Joe was an absolute hit.

But it was Chera and the other Insider girls who saved my ass and kept me sane that winter.

Katie, Megan and Pepper kept us in the advice, fashion and entertainment loops.

Nicole arrived in Dawson that winter, at the proposal of a miner who needed a warm body and a firewood stacker.

When she was booted from her beau's wall tent, Nicole rented Zig's bedroom, keeping me company and helping with odd jobs — searching the clip art bible, photocopying, buying booze.

I co-opted her into writing a few pieces.

Housesitting Blues was a poignant piece inspired by the candles she left burning, both for the miner and in a Yukon Housing duplex she was supposed to be tending.

Thankfully. the small fire was extinguished, as was her love, and they were the subject of her column and not a news story.

One cold January day, I was thrilled to feel my toes tingling, not from frostbite, but from a reader's submission.

I don't remember how it ended up on my desk — if it was mailed in or Chera delivered it, or if I knew at the time who wrote it.

It was a delicious discourse on female angst, voicing "feminine frenzy and fervour" penned by a muse calling herself *There's a Girl on My Tongue*. It was divine.

I was torn. This was fabulous prose, but was it appropriate? Controversial? I was convinced of the artistic integrity, but how did that fit in with journalism?

Her by-line was brilliant, but pure innuendo.

I was the editor and had to make the call.

I desperately wanted to do right by Chris and Zig. For Zig, the bottom line was cash. I don't think he even read most of the stories we published as long as the ads were good and plenty.

But Chris cared about the words. The structure. The scoop! He was a bona fide journalist. I was a just a twenty-something hippy poet chick.

Chris was drowning in the hole that was the *Horse's Mouth*.

I knew that truly doing right by him meant taking the responsibility on my own shoulders. Making the right call. Using my instincts. Not bothering him.

It was remarkable the talent that graced the pages of our little weekly. The unique voices, points of views. I don't think we truly realized at the time the profound magic of the words we published. We were too busy filing them away in search of next week's text.

I printed it. And I asked her to write more.

Zig read it.

Zig read all three columns that *Girl on My Tongue* wrote.

He didn't like what he found. He'd been gone for a few weeks and, without cell phones in those days, we were mostly out of touch. He was far away in Arizona.

When he got back to Dawson City, he said to stop the column.

Zig didn't like the direction the Insider had turned. He wanted his family-friendly TV guide back. He wanted John Wierda to lead the way.

There's a Girl on my Tongue was cut.

Girl was fine with it. She explained just recently how she was in a "life writing" stage and was simply exploring.

Girl got over the axing. So, did I. But Chris didn't.

***

Kim is right. I was mad. Zig only sold five copies of the annual at Quartsite, where publications are always free.

His idea was a bust. He and McNutt ended up selling spinning widgets trailer-to-trailer in order to earn enough gas money to drive back to the Yukon.

The cash was all gone. The credit card was full.

Zig had to make enough money to drive that five thousand kilometres back to the Yukon, where everything was falling apart. He did.

When he got back to Whitehorse, more than a month had passed. We weren't in great shape.

JP had to give up the bedroom to Zig, so he slept under the dining room table. I remember JP used to bring girls back to his semi-private lair while I searched the refrigerator for food. I tried to stay quiet.

The fridge was empty. It was always empty. I didn't hang around in the kitchen much those days.

I remember going to the bar one evening in late February with JP, Josh and Bill, who caused a brawl when he said something to someone that he shouldn't have.

Bill was an occasional writer for the *Horse's Mouth* and spent a lot of time in our office. We knew him well.

Josh and JP were there to back him up in the struggle. It was stupid.

On the way home, post-melee, JP got mad and overtook the wheel while Bill was still driving. He pushed Bill out of the driver's side door, holding on to him just enough to keep Bill's head from hitting the road, just inches away.

JP blamed Bill for the unnecessary bar fight and let him know. He didn't want Bill to be driving and took action. Josh cheered them both on from the back seat.

The *Horse's Mouth* staff had come to blows. Things were not looking good for our operation.

Josh fled Whitehorse for Dawson City soon after, apparently to help Kim and Chera with the Insider.

He abandoned his ad sales responsibilities in Whitehorse. He gave up on The *Horse's Mouth* and left. Nobody was buying ads anyway. Whitehorse business managers all continued to advertise with the *Yukon News*. The TV guide didn't matter to them. Stacks of unsold *Horse's Mouths* sat all over the Takhini North property, adding to the flavour of the failing neighbourhood.

By the end of February, hardly anyone was around. Zig was somewhere on the continent. Josh was gone. Bill never showed his face in the office again.

JP was finding photos and women. I stayed in the basement and just kept putting words together as best I could.

There was no one to sell ads. I had to start dropping writers because there was no money to pay them.

It was a weird existence. We were sinking fast and I was mostly alone. People had stopped dropping by. The phone rang only with complaints from readers wondering why the TV guide sucked so badly.

When Zig finally showed up, he wasn't happy.

He expected success everywhere. He expected the Insider to be humming and the *Horse's Mouth* to be full of advertising.

All he found was an empty ghetto duplex and an exhausted, sad, burnt out editor who wanted to be in Dawson.

Zig disagreed with our decision to run *Girl*. He disagreed with lots of stuff. Suddenly, we weren't getting along. His exuberance had worn off. I was angry. So was he. We were broke.

I didn't trust him anymore and he didn't trust me.

Zig rewrote an editorial in an early March Insider because he disagreed with what I had to say. He made the decision unilaterally. I was done.

Kim puts it succinctly: "We were a family right through Christmas. That changed by March. The trust was gone."

I packed my bag and left in early March. I quit Whitehorse. I quit the *Horse's Mouth*. I headed back to Dawson with D in McNutt's borrowed car that broke down on the way.

I wrote an editorial for the Insider that thanked the generous mechanic who helped us roadside to get us safely back to Dawson City, no time nor limbs lost.

Then I laid down and did not move until the end of April — five weeks of bedrest back at the house I had rented with D in December. The last ten months had caught up with me. I had hit complete exhaustion. D looked after me. Julie let me stay. Django protected me.

Kim plugged away at the Insider for a couple more weeks. Josh was in her way. She doesn't know why he came back to Dawson. Kim thinks he was chasing her helper, Nicole. He didn't help her at all.

By April 1, Kim was done, too. She was concerned that Zig couldn't pay her anymore and accepted another job offer.

She remembers nothing about March except the phone bill — she had forgotten to change the ISP over from Whitehorse to Dawson one day that January.

Each time she was on the internet, she was dialling long distance. The bill was enormous, and Zig hit the roof when it was discovered. I think the bill was over one thousand dollars simply for connecting to the internet. Times have certainly changed.

The failure in Whitehorse was spectacular and complete. The *Horse's Mouth* lasted one more issue and was then laid to rest. I had no part of it.

JP was the last man standing in the ghetto.

When the heating fuel finally ran out on him, he abandoned the *Horse's Mouth* house and followed us to Dawson, where he continued to chase girls and take photos for a few more months. I have no idea what happened to the stacks of unsold *Horse's Mouths*.

We were broke. The credit card was full. We had debt everywhere and no cash. In just one month, we had to print one hundred thousand copies of the annual. But that printing money was gone. I was too exhausted to care. It was no longer my problem.

Chapter 18
Dawson City Revival

Tim was returning from his bicycle trip and he wanted his house back. I had to figure life out very quickly.

Julie, D and I had to move out by the end of April.

I elected to move into a rented wall tent across the Klondike River from Dawson City back in Lousetown, where I had previously lived in the abandoned camper.

I bought a fifty dollar "hippy killer" wood stove to keep me from freezing at night. I remember it glowed like an overheated tin can as the thin metal quickly melted away. The stove was simply not skookum enough for the cold temperatures of a Klondike spring. I used to watch sparks fly through the metal. Still, it was better than freezing. The stove was well named.

JP and I had both adopted puppies that month and we wanted open ground to raise them. I named mine Typo. He named his Ronin, the masterless warrior. Lousetown was a great place to let puppies run and play. They both lived for many years.

D found housing in the Klondike Valley with a friend. She and I had broken off our relationship and were going our separate ways. She wanted me to commit. I wasn't so sure of anything at that time. It was sad.

Julie (and there's a reason she's in this story), came up with a great plan for a new roomie.

She imported Stef from Montreal. With one phone call, she changed the fortunes of the Dawson City Insider.

Stef got on the bus in Montreal. He put his Macintosh G3 tower in his lap and did not let it go until he was in Dawson City, some six thousand kilometres away.

Stef was educated in the science of water, but the computer was his true passion. He was enthralled with the publishing and printing industry.

He loved the mechanics of it; a smooth running of the bells and whistles that make it all click behind the scenes is what Stef brings to this world. That, and a wonderful broken English that is heavily accented with a deep, Quebecois accent.

Did I mention he was the face of the Stand-in Bartender when Katie couldn't come through?

Wayne Potoroka would take over the advice column, writing in Stef's muddled English and techie leave-me-alone attitude. Stef is no bartender.

Julie had sent Stef to meet Zig at the Klassic within a day of his arrival. She told him to go find a job and start there.

Zig and Stef were a perfect match.

Zig badly needed someone to get his computer equipment, his software, his filing system all running up to speed. He also needed someone to train him on font suitcases and effective "etherneting".

Stef needed the work.

Chera continued to show up to the Klassic, business as usual. Looking back, Chera was the glue that kept the business from failing in March 1998.

She never quit. She just kept showing up at the Klassic and producing great ads. She helped Zig figure out the problems while I convalesced. She made all the difference.

Chera still plugs away as a graphic artist in her home studio somewhere south of Whitehorse, designing mostly for those clients that can afford her.

I stayed away from the office. I didn't have any plans for the future, and I didn't want to look at the past. I simply wanted to stay in bed and rest.

But towards the end of April, my positive attitude returned. I wanted to get life going again. I started to think more about my successes than my failures in the last year. I felt a responsibility to complete the annual. I went back to the Klassic.

The office was humming! Zig had put the *Horse's Mouth* failure behind him. He had shut the Insider down for the time being. He was focused on getting the 1998 annual published. He had not given up. Stef and Chera were working hard.

I recognized this energy. Spring was in the air; the sun was once again high in the sky and the smell of money came with it. The Klassic had warmed with the returning sun and was once again a busy publishing office.

I couldn't help but smile and be attracted to the energy. The nightmare of the *Horse's Mouth* was fading fast. It was time Zig and I had a sit down. We had a lot to discuss. We talked openly for about an hour. By the end of it, we were laughing. He needed my help to finish the annual. I needed to do something.

I was no longer angry. During my long rest, I accepted my role in the failure of the Whitehorse expansion and wanted to make amends. I agreed to work for a little more than peanuts to bring us back out of debt. I wanted to be responsible.

I agreed to work for two hundred dollars a week as long as Zig paid off the debt, especially the printing debt with Steve Robertson at the *Yukon News*. I think it was around five thousand dollars.

That debt irked me for some reason. I wanted Steve to think well of us. It was a big deal to me because I had once worked for the *Yukon News*. I respected him a lot. I wanted him to respect me. I wanted to be reliable.

I told Zig that I would help him finish the annual if he re-started the Insider in May and paid off what we owed Steve by the end of the summer.

I reminded him how much money the Insider made before our unceremonious fall from grace the previous winter. I reminded him that the Insider actually made it through the winter, despite the disaster of the *Horse's Mouth*.

I also negotiated for proper office space. It was time to get out of the Klassic. I didn't want to be there anymore.

Zig agreed to all this. He promised to find us new space. He promised to pay off Steve. He promised we would restart the Insider.

I promised to avoid eroticism between the ads. That's what Zig wanted most from me – no more controversy.

We agreed. I went back to work.

Let's look deep into my big blue bin again to reveal more of the past and see how this story ends. I have no newspapers for March 1998. I know we published, but outside of a couple of terrible editorials, I didn't write.

In April, we published just once. We successfully put together a fantastic, money making annual. Zig deferred payment of the printing bill for ninety days. Spending all the printing money months earlier to support our growth really wasn't a big deal in the end. It's just business. I didn't have to worry so much.

The next issue I dig out is for May 12th, 1998 — the Insider was back in business.

The headline screams: "Hotel Numbers Way Up For Summer!"

And they were.

The one hundredth anniversary of the Klondike gold rush was in 1998. The Yukon had big plans to celebrate and Dawson City was the centre of it all.

If you have never heard of this crazy gold rush, well, you should. Pierre Berton's *Klondike* is an amazing read. It details in full glory the world-wide stampede to the Yukon in the quest for Klondike gold. It's one of the best non-fiction books ever put together.

People flocked to the Yukon to retrace the steps their ancestors took and to see what the noise was all about.

Clients once again began knocking on our door. They wanted to take advantage of the anniversary celebrations.

Most didn't know the Insider had even shut down.

The ones that knew didn't care. Nobody was around in April, anyway. May had arrived! Summer was starting and everyone was looking to make money. It was a complete antithesis to what I had experienced through the long, dark, cold months in the *Horse's Mouth* ghetto basement.

A year had passed since I arrived to help Zig. It seemed like a century. We were so much smarter. We were organized. We had Chera. We had Stef. We had clients that believed in us and we had a new work environment.

Zig rented an entire deserted grocery store for an office. We had all the space we wanted. It was in the heart of town and it even had water!

The columnists were returning as well: *The Bartender*, Wayne, Joe, John, some new folks. Kim wrote a weekly column while working at another job.

The mosquitos were getting to me at the wall tent in Lousetown. The woodstove had disintegrated. Typo and I moved in with D. I accepted her challenge of commitment.

JP spent part of the summer working then got chased out of town by a girl hot on his heels.

Josh disappeared entirely.

I worked hard but not stupid that spring. I had a golf membership. I walked my dog regularly. I ate. I loved. I found a way back to health in body, soul and mind.

I got engaged the night that the Yukon celebrated its one hundredth birthday at the Klondike Centennial ball. D was the only one wearing a gold dress. I wore a tuxedo. She said yes in the upper balcony of the Palace Grande Theatre. She was gorgeous.

Saturday was the only night of the week I worked late, mostly waiting for the arrival of the *Market Report*.

Today, I look back at those Saturday nights as the fondest of my career. The office was empty. Chera had all the ad changes completed. Most of the stories would have been finished. Columnists usually filed on time. CBC Radio kept me company late into the night when they didn't.

I would put all the pieces of the Insider together, slowly, purposefully and with love, then head to The Pit for a rewarding beer. It was good times.

Zig was mostly on the road chasing ad money for his growing annual. He stayed out of the office and we were better for it. We had no more steps backwards.

Cheques came in hand over fist, filling the mailbox. The bank account ballooned again. We even won a major national bank award — Under 30 Entrepreneurs of the Year for the Yukon awarded by the Canadian government's Business Development Bank. It was a big deal.

Zig bought us used laptops so we could work on the road without packing up half the office. It was the first time I had ever used a laptop. What a change to my world.

Stef made sure everything ran smoothly.

We had all the pieces in place for success by simply staying in Dawson and sharing our messages with the world. We didn't have to expand. We didn't have to go looking. We could work seasonally then shut down for a few months and travel if we wished.

We had overcome all the problems. We had a great team at the right place at the right time. It was the perfect environment, the perfect people, the perfect work world.

So why did it all have to end?

Chapter 19
Unraveled

By June 1998, we were beyond humming. Everybody was buying something from us. Advertising was selling for the Insider, which expanded to twenty-four pages. The annual, and the annual in German, were already selling out for 1999. Desktop publishing filled in the rest of the work hours. Even Stef jumped in to do graphic art. This thing called web design was starting to be discussed.

Still, we all found time to rest — there was to be no more burnout, no more all-nighters.

None of us worked overtime anymore and we made far more money than the previous year. The operation had been streamlined. Zig managed the business from his laptop. He was no longer allowed on the production computers. That was an essential part of the streamlining process.

As much as we loved him, we all knew it was Zig who often took us that one step back Kim mentioned.

He just couldn't resist tinkering with the computers. He would install new fonts, partition hard drives, turn Suitcase on and off, throw out files to create space for new ones, change the template for the Insider and add new programs. Zig learned through trial and error. There were no manuals and little planning in his world.

He would do this without telling anyone. And often, bad things would happen, sucking time. Files that Chera had worked on for hours would be gone when she turned on the computer the next morning. Sometimes a computer wouldn't turn on at all. Or if it did, the hard drive would stop spinning, the clock of trouble would show up onscreen and start to turn, followed by the black screen of death.

Tech would be called. I remember Chera's voice clearly: "Stef? Can you come over? The computer is dead again."

Stef would take over; push a few keys and she would be back in business.

Long sighs of knowing would follow: Zig had been in the office. He always meant well. He just loved to experiment. Chera rarely lost her temper. Zig would again be banned. He wasn't mad about it. He'd laugh and grab a broom, relegated to sweeping.

The cycle would repeat but there was so much money pouring in and Zig was great with the clients. It was hard to remain frustrated.

I look at the front-page headlines for those early summer 1998 issues. They are mostly bland. No more dead bears and no more missing canoeists.

Even the price of gold had become stable.

I'm not sure if the reporting had become less adventurous or if there were no stories to tell in Dawson.

I think it was the reporting.

The Insider was missing Kim's stories. She was only writing a column called, *More to life than coffee*. Her first column discussed the differences between West Best and Pepsi Colas. Yawn.

People opened up to Kim. They often asked about her. They didn't care about her Cola thoughts. They wanted her hard stories. Kim wrote a few more columns that summer then faded away from the pages. It was sad.

In an early May *Market Report*, Wayne discussed the waste of time necessitated by listening to people recount their dreams. Double yawn.

The Insider was publishing upbeat and simple. This was Zig's direction to get us back into profitability. There was to be no more hounding government officials. There was to be no more Klondike erotica.

The Insider was avoiding conflict and controversy. Compared to the summer before, when Kim and I were nailing politicians to the cross whenever we could, it was soft.

One front-page headline reads, "Panning Championships Highlight Holidays". What a snoozer. That one hurts.

My editorials mostly cheered on Dawson. They no longer pointed long, knowing fingers at failed policy or compulsive politicians. The Insider was happy and friendly. I had sold out.

There was the odd news story: local vandalism, families needing help after a fire, a break-in, but mostly, I ran stories about new businesses opening and about how busy the town was. Boring.

Still, controversies brewed and bubbled over. The Insider couldn't avoid them because they found us. We were a newspaper when newspapers were still relevant.

Larry Vezina had invested hundreds of thousands of dollars into developing variety shows for the town's two entertainment venues: Diamond Tooth Gertie's Casino and the Palace Grande Theatre.

Both venues entertained tourists with live music and dance acts that celebrated Dawson City's gold rush history.

Vezina had a three-year contract with the Klondike Visitor's Association, which managed the shows for both facilities. That contract was open for renewal each year through a bidding process. The KVA wanted the contractor to be accountable each season.

Vezina was about to enter the third year of producing the shows when the KVA pulled the plug on him.

He lost the contract when another company undercut his bid by more than two hundred and fifty thousand dollars.

Vezina was hopping mad. He had "invested a lifetime" into the shows and wanted his return in the third year. He vented to me about the losses he would incur.

The KVA never relented. The shows were contracted out to Lorraine Butler, who had moved her act to Dawson from the south, where she operated a very similar show.

I had heard whispers of disaster about the show. For the June 2, 1998, editorial, I decided to see the show myself.

Let's see what I had to say.

An Insider's View
By Chris Beacom

Last week I heard oodles of opinions about this year's KVA shows. Everywhere I turned, I heard something about them. Two weeks ago, I figured I'd run a promo piece and move on. I wouldn't review them because I know as much about song and dance as I do about Guatemala (not much).

Well, that's changed. With all the talk about the shows, I thought I'd better go see for myself what the hype's all about. The KVA shows are critical to our economy now. Tourism is everything and the KVA is in the centre of it all. If word gets out that our shows are weak, everyone suffers. This is important; no use hiding my head in the printer's ink.

On with the show…

Gaslight Follies: 13 songs, 3 tap dances, gorgeous set, sparkling costumes, Rosemary Raspberry rocks, moderately funny, cheap sex jokes, the theatre is always stifling, a woman wiped out on the steps. I went to

Kate's for a cold one between shows, 90 minutes, pretty girls, only one instrument, people are brought back to the turn of the century (it's not referred to). No problem.

Diamond Tooth Gerties: three acts, only saw one (didn't want to see anymore), dancers were different heights and not in sync, sound was awful, lighting was flat, songs were all similar, a lack of can-can, friends lost interest in under three minutes and returned to conversation, I lost $20 at the tables, alcohol was expensive, people bailed after the second show, Steve wasn't making any tips. Some problems, but hopefully they can be overcome.

The KVA and the shows are terrific, and any problems are a minor concern. Gertie said everything is fine and she is getting rave reviews. I hope it's true. Personal pride and small-town politics are irrelevant when the entire town's economy is at stake.

***

The KVA had been on my radar since 1994, when an employee of the unionized casino had complained to Caroline Murray at the *Klondike Sun* that the boss had requested her to "sew boobs into her dress."

Murray's story ran front page. The boss had been fired after the next edition was printed. No boobs were ever sewn. It was a win for journalism.

Diamond Tooth Gertie's casino was started in 1971 by the non-profit KVA as Canada's first legal gambling house in over 50 years. Thousands of dollars rolled through the casino daily in 1998.

Diamond Tooth Gertie's and the KVA had developed a model that ensured revenue sharing between non-profit organizations, the Yukon government and the casino operator. Most of the workers were unionized.

Unfortunately, the 1998 show really was terrible. It was my responsibility to let people know. My tepid editorial worked! A week later, Vezina was actually contracted by the KVA to help fix the shows before the tourism season went into full swing.

The boss of the KVA even paid me a little visit. He said change was in the air. In the June 30th Insider, a long letter written on behalf of the KVA explained how the shows were being overhauled. The Insider had done its job. I had done my job. Journalism was once again making a difference in the Klondike.

Let's go back to the big blue bin and see how the summer of 1998 unfolded. I notice that I'm starting to get near the bottom of the pile.

Let's peruse the headlines.

Sarah Winton's letter campaign prevented Dawson City council from imposing a draconian bylaw that would have all youth under a curfew because of isolated, late-night vandalism. The teenager also argued her case in front of the council, informing them of the error of such measures. The council relented. The motion was tossed out.

It was a great win for youth. The Insider was there and covered it all. There would be no mandatory curfew for anyone in Dawson.

Aedes Scheer took a permanent break from her veterinary technician job after four gruelling years to further her education. The Insider reported how a new veterinarian was coming to town and thanked Scheer for her service on behalf of all Klondikers.

John Wierda was still giving financial advice.

Famous musician Nathan Tinkham was playing for the summer at the Westminster Hotel and wrote a column called *A view from The Pit*.

RCMP Corporal Tim Bain's "name and shame" column was a real hindrance to criminal activity. No one in town wanted to end up in Bain's column.

Joe Urie had traded in his Ron and Don theme for a summer column called *From the Deathbed of Joe Urie — Cheap Hack*. He was taking his writing, and town issues, more seriously. It was Ron Cherry well beyond hockey.

The *Market Report* continued, so did the *Bartender*, so did the TV guide.

There was the mundane side as well: our dentist had returned; the local planning board had a new staff member. How standard. How normal. How boring.

What's this? An interesting letter from June 9, 1998. I could always count on Mayor Glen Everitt to spice up the Insider. I didn't even have to go digging for the story. Never far from the spotlight, Everitt showed his anger at the federal (Liberal) government and he chose the Insider to voice his opinion.

Let's have a read:

Dear Editor,

The Manager of Federal Water Resources, Dave Sherstone, owes Dawson residents an apology.

On June 2, 1998, CBC reported that the City of Dawson has provided information to prove that they are not causing damage to the habitat of the Yukon River with their sewage, nor is there any health risk to the people of the Klondike.

I am absolutely astounded at the comments of Dave Sherstone, Federal Water Resource Manager.

He had implied, with his comments, that residents of the Klondike pour paint, PCBs, toxin and furan containing ballast fluids from transformers into their toilets.

These comments are out of line for a federal public servant.

To fabricate and imply that the residents of my community would adhere to such negative environmental habits is a slap in the face and won't be tolerated.

These comments more than confirm that the strategy used by the department is not to provide scientific proof, but to create rumour to gain public support.

I request a retraction of your comments and an apology to the people of the Klondike.

Dawson City, in partnership with the territorial government, has developed a comprehensive plan, not to mention has created a land fill site, with storage available for all hazardous materials.

Of course, if your department would become more service-oriented and research the communities it represents, it would know that.

Mayor Glen Everitt

Dawson City

***

Hello sexy story number two!

Dawson's mayor had just called out a high level, federal bureaucrat in our pages.

I remember pouring trays of discarded film processing fluid down the drain at the *Klondike Sun* in 1994 that went straight into the Yukon River.

I also once unknowingly picked up a burlap bag of dead puppies from the shoreline of that same river.

I knew the Yukon River had been a dumping ground since the gold rush. But the river was massive, swelling to hold the water of many rivers heading north and west to the Bering Sea by the time it passed tiny Dawson City. Whatever the locals decided to put into that river probably didn't affect it. There was simply too much water and not enough people.

This story had sides. It had drama. It had long legs to help it run, I was about to learn.

So was Wayne Potoroka.

He had taken the summer off work to figure out his future and play golf.

Potoroka was also enthralled by Everitt's letter. He wanted to learn more about the Yukon River. He decided to write a bunch of articles for the Insider. He didn't like the soft direction the Insider was taking and wanted to roll up his sleeves and tackle some tough issues. In the July 14, 1998 edition, Potoroka became political.

Potoroka wanted to know what was happening to the Yukon River salmon. He wanted to know why the number of salmon swimming the river was dwindling. He talked to government officials, conservation folks and fishers to find answers.

He learned overfishing in international Pacific waters was wiping out the returns. The fish weren't making it up the Yukon River in any numbers to feed the Tr'ondëk Hwëch'in, who had lived off the salmon for millennia. They still aren't returning. There are even fewer fish today.

But Potoroka's research went even deeper.

By August 11, Wayne was in the town's tertiary water screening plant, staring down at the powerful Yukon River water pumping through it at a remarkable force.

A series of screens kept unwanted objects out of the river, though they did nothing about unwanted fluids or coliforms (bacteria). A set of false teeth sat among other objects that had been taken out of the screens and saved. Potoroka loved it. A photo of the teeth ran with his story.

Peter Jenkins had overseen the construction of the screening plant when the dyke was built after the 1979 flood. He stood by the plant's effectiveness for his entire political career.

Wayne wanted to know if the plant was truly effective. He wanted to know why Everitt was so outraged with the federal government, which had been fine with the screening plant based on regular testing of treated and untreated Yukon River water for almost two decades.

But the feds changed their opinion in the 1990s and started to push local government officials to build a wastewater treatment plant to replace the screening plant. Whether it was needed in Dawson or not, a new wastewater facility would serve as a legal precedent to build similar plants in other jurisdictions.

One test result in 1998 put politics ahead of science.

The LC50 test determines whether water is clean enough to sustain life by measuring how many fish live in a bucket of unoxygenated water for ninety-six hours. If the fish live, the water is safe. If they die, the water is considered not safe. If some fish live and some do not, then the findings are debatable.

Did the scientists scoop up a few fish with a bunch of Yukon River water to be tested in the LC50 bucket as it flew down to Vancouver? Or did they fly a bucket of water directly from the screening plant to Vancouver and deposit some local fish into the bucket for ninety-six hours? The answer is not clear. The facts are murky around the actual test. Either way, the fish died in the bucket.

Based on this failed test, the federal government decided a new multi-million-dollar sewage treatment plant was required. They used the results from this questionable test, performed only once, to push their agenda.

The federal government never apologized to Everitt. The town council never backed down on the efficiency of its current treatment plant.

The feds used these dead fish as their only evidence at that December's water board hearings, and in later court hearings, to eventually force a court order on Dawson to have a secondary sewage treatment plant built.

An independent scientist at those hearings pointed out that no sewage was discernible on any spot in the Yukon River more than twenty-five meters downstream from the outlet pipe. The feds ignored the independent science. The town ignored the feds. A year later, the feds stormed the town's offices and took away computers as evidence. The fight was truly on. The

Insider covered the entire water board license hearing. It was a great story. It is a great story.

Eventually, the Yukon government took over the project on behalf of the town. It abided by a territorial court order and built the new plant. It took fourteen years before it was finally constructed. Dawson's battles continued however, as the territorial government ignored the town's advice about the design of the project.

That was a mistake. The new sewage plant failed swiftly and miserably because there was not enough sewage to keep it running efficiently in cold temperatures. Dawson City is just too small to keep it going. The town doesn't generate enough waste for it to break down effectively. The Yukon government was told this was a risk by the town. They built the new plant anyway. It failed immediately.

Sewage backups in both the new treatment plant in 2013, and the old screening plant in 2014, have forced all the governments to rethink their future Klondike sewage solutions.

"Seventeen feet of shit water," Potoroka explained to me flatly one day about the incidents that resulted in untreated sewage pouring into Dawson City streets at sub-zero temperatures.

I see Potoroka now and then. I go up to visit Dawson when I can. As mayor, he's still on the official sewage beat for the town. He hasn't given up. He keeps me up to date. We talk sewage today like it's a half-eaten sandwich we continue to share. The story's legs keep getting longer. I keep paying attention. He keeps building.

The Yukon government is now building its second new sewage plant – a lagoon system at the front of town. It's expected to be completed in 2026. Territorial officials are now listening to the municipality about the design and location.

Potoroka says there is no way the town could go back to running just the old screening plant.

"It's socially unacceptable in this day and age not to have secondary sewage treatment."

But taxpayers are still on the hook for more than forty million dollars, over twenty years, on a highly questionable project that was decided based on measuring the lifespan of a few fish stuck in a bucket. It's a boondoggle of the highest order. It's a government disaster at all levels. It's a continuing great story.

Let's look back to August 1998. Sewage wasn't the only controversy that summer.

More letters were printed back and forth about the KVA shows; how they sucked or didn't suck, and why. This trend continued for the entire summer.

The Insider front page story on August 11 explained how KVA revenues were down three hundred thousand dollars from the previous year. The KVA was considering cancelling the Palace Grande show in future years. They did. It's been cancelled for decades. How tragic.

Letters filled the front pages of the newspaper. People wanted their say. They would call each other out. The Insider was like Facebook of 1998 in the Klondike.

I was continually hounded about choosing to run letters or not. We ran controversial, passionate pieces and people were responding with their own opinions. It was tit for tat.

I didn't need to search out more catchy headlines to spice up the Insider — the readers were bringing it all to me.

I flip through these old papers now and see I had to apologize in the Insider about something or other more than once that summer. I loved being an editor. Readers were bringing controversy to the Insider and I was responding. I was doing my job.

The Insider had become an established newspaper. The *Klondike Sun*, which was printed twice a month, was suffering. All the ad dollars were flowing our way. I started to feel sympathy for them.

On September 8, I wrote an *Insider's View* about how I had the best job on the planet; about how much I loved the Insider.

It was the last newsprint Insider I ever created.

On September 13, 1998, D and I got married. It was a big party held at a special spot. Django and Typo were at the altar. JP was best man. He returned to Dawson just for the occasion.

It was a new beginning for us, and the beginning of the end for the Insider.

Zig decided after that week that the Insider would no longer run on newsprint. He didn't want the expense. He didn't want another winter of hell.

The photocopier was to be put back into business for the next few months. Stef mastered the automatic paper folder Zig purchased to save on labor.

I still remember Stef spraying Static Guard onto the paper folder out of an aerosol can each week to keep the pages from sticking together while cursing in French. The machine got so hot, I feared it would catch fire and ignite the spray. But Stef never caught on fire. We never blew up.

Zig said we were going to save money by going back to the photocopier, though I didn't see how.

I agreed to the change, reluctantly and with sadness. I hated going back. I saw the beginning of a trend with Zig.

I continued to write, but people were not happy with the change. They wanted their weekly newspaper. They didn't want a photocopy. They didn't want us to go backwards. Advertisers complained, then tailed off. Letters dwindled.

Autumn arrived and we worked diligently on the annual. Zig argued correctly that there was simply more money to be made with it than with the Insider.

The little weekly newspaper that could was starting to become forgotten.

The *Klondike Sun* won the battle simply by remaining consistent. It's still in operation today.

I focused my time on filling and editing both the Insider and the annual, but my heart wasn't into it.

I asked Zig about the finances. I had promised to work that summer for two hundred dollars a week in order to pay off all corporate debt with that amazing run of cheques filling our mailbox.

With a new wife and a life to build for both of us, it was time to check in. I needed to make a living wage.

Zig said there wasn't any money around even though we'd earned tens of thousands of dollars that summer. He said he had paid off the outstanding printing bill for the annual, though he wasn't quite sure. He said we were still behind, despite the money flowing in.

He didn't offer me any more money. He also hadn't yet paid back the *Yukon News*.

Ah, there was the rub.

We weren't going to print the Insider anymore because he still owed Steve Robertson money for printing the *Horse's Mouth*.

Zig wasn't hiding money, nor was he holding out. I don't think he was dishonest or greedy. He simply did not have the financial management skills at that time to control the money flow. Money was moving in too quickly from too many different directions; in from hundreds of clients, out to dozens of bills. It was a lot to manage. I was not surprised. It didn't matter.

My terms for returning to work that April had not been met. It was time to go. Despite all the success that summer, I never saw myself making more than two hundred dollars a week with Zig. It was time to leave Dawson.

D and I stayed until March 1999. Until we left, Zig and I finished another successful annual, we attended awards ceremonies and we made money.

In January 1999, Zig no longer wanted the office. The Insider shut down for the winter as a cost control measure. I helped Zig move the equipment back to the Klassic. The photocopier was returned to its familiar position. Zig's dog went back under the desk.

It was a really sad day.

The team faded and so did the Insider. My big blue bin keeps it from disappearing entirely. Everybody went their separate ways.

Years later, I'd like to thank them all.

I'd like to thank Chera for her many hours making the Insider advertising look so good and for keeping the operation running through her consistency.

I'd like to thank Kim for lighting the fires that keep good journalism going even today.

I'd like to thank Joe, Wayne, Katie, Girl on my Tongue, Pepper, Wills, Megan, Katie, the corporal and John for all the columns.

I'd like to thank the other writers in Dawson and Whitehorse, from Nathan Tinkham to our only French writer, Yves Bellavance, to Chris Dorey, who rocked as an early "What to do in Dawson" columnist. There are too many of you to mention one by one.

I'd like to thank the people of Dawson City and Whitehorse for reading.

I'd like to thank Dom for his editing and humour that first summer.

I'd like to thank Josh and JP for trying.

I'd like to thank Lenart for his patience.

I'd like to thank Paulette for making the *Horse's Mouth* look better than it was.

I'd like to thank Stef for fixing everything.

I'd like to thank Nicole for helping Kim out during that horrific January 1998.

I'd like to thank Bill for always stopping by.

I'd like to thank Zig for the opportunity and the many Yukon adventures – it was exactly what I was looking for. I hope everyone lives well.

The Insiders are still here, filling my big blue bin after twenty-plus years of keeping them safe. I'm happy to share them now. They have fulfilled their role. I am tired of carting them around from place to place.

I can share an article or two, an ad from the day, a photo from the past or a whole issue. I just have to take a picture of a page with my cell phone and hit send. It's easy.

It is so not 1997.

The stories will be shared; history can be revisited.

The Insider can live on, just ask.

After all, it's free.

RIVERWEST FOOD AND HEALTH COFFEE CLUB

NATURAL (BULK) FOODS	MONDAY-SATURDAY 8 A.M. TO 8 P.M.
SOY PRODUCTS • VITAMINS • BODY CARE	SUNDAY 10 A.M. TO 6 P.M.
ALPINE BAKERY BREAD	ENTER OUR WEEKLY DRAW

THIS WEEK'S WINNER IS: LOLITA WELCHMAN

MONDAY, JUNE 23RD, 1997

DAWSON CITY INSIDER

ALL THE NEWS THAT'S FIT TO PRINT

FIRE DESTROYS ANOTHER DAWSON BUSINESS

A fire struck Arctic Drugs last Tuesday afternoon. At time of print, the cause of the blaze and extent of damage were not made available to the public.

The R.C.M.P. and Dawson City Fire Department Chief Pat Cayen were investigating the fire Wednesday afternoon. Cayen was not available for comment. Arctic Drugs owner Fred Berger also refused comment regarding the fire.

Over 100 people gathered on the street witnessed smoke escaping from the roof. Flames were not visible as fire crews kept them confined to the building's interior.

KLONDIKE KATE'S

7am – 11 pm Daily

Full Service Restaurant
Clean, Affordable Accommodation
Espressos & Lattes

Breakfast Special ~ $3.99
Located on Historic King and 3rd

MAXIMILIAN'S

• Newspapers • Books
• Magazines • Tapes & CDs
• Tobacco
• Fresh Plants Every Friday
• One dozen roses
$39.95

The first issue of the Dawson City Insider, June 23, 1997. Through new digital technology, a small rookie team was able to create the town's first weekly newspaper in over forty years. A fire broke out just before deadline, providing a last-minute front-page story.

Kim Favreau hunts down a story for the
Dawson City Insider in 1997.

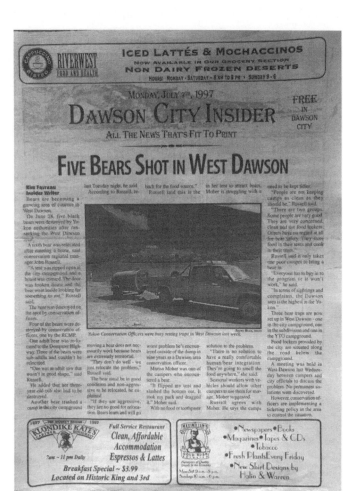

Five dead bears shot and killed by Yukon government conservation officers was a necessary action, they said, to prevent bears from attacking campers in Tent City.

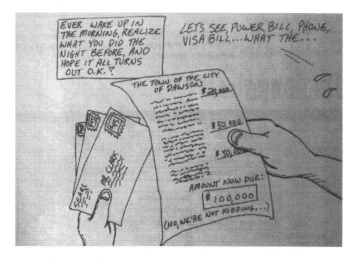

Insider cartoonist Adam Larson captures Dawson mayor Glen Everitt's effort to bill BC premier Glen Clark one hundred thousand dollars for missed tourism dollars because of a ferry blockade in the Pacific Ocean.

Django, the Klondike's meanest dog for fifteen years.

The first issue of the *Horse's Mouth* entertainment
guide published in Whitehorse in January 1998.

HER SIDE: THE STORY OF NO

I WEPT AND I WALKED AND THE CLOUDS CLEARED FROM THE SKY AND I THOUGHT MAYBE ...

Alas, it has befallen. My love lust caisserole had an obtrusive consummation.

Another Saturday night, another encrusted fantasy. She took the wound deeply into her heart. Standing tall and fearless against the dagger. Wavering only when lust blood swamped the linoleum and her slippers slid from under her. She tumbled heavily onto the forlorn coach.

The T.V. is not quite annoying enough to turn off. My eyes aren't quite tired enough to close. I covet the cadaver of my fictitious girl.

The woman on channel 2 with the spiral perm is telling me how she met the person of her dreams through a video dating service.

Imagination rescues the mortal.

The night takes me closer to it as I enter sleep and leave the evening's deluge of dejection to memory.

A venomous tincture of fantasy and reality. Everything is so perfectly placed...until... tangible form makes it all slippery, and phlegmatic it falls from her hands.

I watch it dissipate into the murk of the smoky room. The night doesn't end when it doesn't come true.

I curtail the misty remnants of my romantic invention and leave the love passion energy to create new dance steps, exhausting the rejection.

Tomorrow, a virgin illusion will undoubtedly bloom from my aching loins. The dominae hormone swipes, consuming my body/mind. Luring me though days of the unrest.

Another chapter to burn in her bed sheets. Alone she'll sweat and squirm. Until one day she walks out the door with it. As expectant as a parturient woman.

The girl on the T.V. is wearing a red sequined mini-skirt and a black push-up bra. She gyrates beside her interviewer, who leans into her and asks, "What do you look for in a mate?"

She retorts, "I look for someone who's tall, blond, muscular, and into having a good time."

Dare she tempt to satiate her desires....

Lovingly,

There's a girl in my teacup

HOUSE-SITTING BLUES

Nicole Wasurchak
Insider Writer

My body feels manipulated by the aches in my muscles and the bruises upon my ego. Facial soaring of tension and pent-up aggression leaves me less than appealing inside my mind's eye. An erotic witch doctor is the only one I believe who can save me now. I call upon the spirits, but summon them, I cannot. They're too tired to deal with me. I'm on my own. Karma? Irides-cent energy? Is that what is backlashing full throttle at me? Caused me to become an arsonist-by-accident in an unknown someone's home? Unwanted house guest or irresponsibility, it's a tough call at this point. Maybe some of all, perhaps none of the above. Could be lack of the ever-precious sleep components that has caused the window to crash down at my hate feet. Or it could be that the smell of burning sweet grass reminds me of such other pleasures that I enjoy, and that is why I am left with nothing but a pile of ash and a broken racisum. Maybe it was the request/warning I received before claiming the throne as my own. "A cheap replacement" echoes in my ears from the hollow sounds in the wall. Nothing makes any bit of rational sense and

I am afraid of how it would sound if it did come with it's own explanation typed on a slip of tiny paper and folded inside a sigh, a hide inside a fortune cookie. I'd be afraid to confront the genius of the destiny. I have claiming and feel open and geeked up greedily just 'cuz. I can't seem to be satisfied with my own. I stand away at the charred embers and molten plastic, and it takes my back to the time I melted my school friend's toys in her Little Miss Easy Suzy Bake oven. I guess it's finally caught up to me and it's my time to clean up the mess. Funny how some things never die, and how some times can never be swept away under the rug, shoved in the corner, or blamed on my invisible friend Jake. Could be it really is all his fault, and since I've become too boring to play his games anymore, he's reinforcing that he can still make me jump quick and can still make my life hell in the flick of the candle wick. I will seek Jake's face out in the crowd. I promised my first offspring would be his in exchange for the escape. As the clock ticks on I begin to worry that I may have made an offer I can't create in reality and he will pack his bags and find a new home to destroy.

Author Chris Ross walks Ronin and Typo to his wall
tent in Lousetown outside of Dawson City, Yukon in
April 1998.

Author Chris Ross' wall tent in Lousetown just before it was demolished in May 1998. The land has since been returned to the Tr'öndek Hwëch'in First Nation and no structures are in the area today.

TUESDAY, MAY 12TH   FREE!

DAWSON CITY INSIDER

MORE MILES THAN MINUTES

Hotel Numbers Way Up for Summer

Chris Benson
Insider Staff

Local hotel managers are pleased with their bookings for the last arriving tourist season.

Downtown Hotel owner Dick Van Nostrand, who also serves as KVA Chairman and President of the Dawson City Chamber of Commerce, said bookings for the dry hotel are way up for the summer.

"We'll be up over last year substantially. We're up over '96 even, and that was the best year so far."

Tour companies such as Holland America, Princess Tours and Horizon start in early June, and Van Nostrand said the cancellation rate is really low.

"The summer staff is not dropping ... The only problem is we have a 100 day season."

With the downturn in mining, Van Nostrand said the local economy has suffered and business in the Downtown Hotel is less this spring than usual.

"Spring has been very slow. The fall was a disaster financially and this year (the fall) will be as well."

As new chairman of the KVA, Van Nostrand said bookings for the Palace Grand are also up substantially from last year.

Although hotel bookings have increased significantly, and the KVA is working in con-

junction with the city and the chamber to deal with a lack of hotel rooms during parts of the summer, Van Nostrand said the hotels are not booked solid yet.

"There are still rooms left in Dawson City," he said.

Westmark Manager Lloyd Robinson confirmed that the hotel's numbers are also back up to the record-setting numbers of 1996. The hotel is up 3,000 booked rooms over last year, and another 1,000 bookings have been sent to other hotels in town.

Another 200 Westmark rooms have been booked for promotional visits to "fam" tours for tourism agents next week. Robinson says these are important to promoting future tourism in Dawson.

"This really does promote Dawson - everybody picks up from these travel agents," she said.

The fall tours start arriving May 23, and from then on, Robinson said the hotel is booked.

"We're very happy - We're just waiting for them."

Triple J manager Darlene Doerksen echoed Robinson's and van Nostrand's sentiments about the coming season.

"It's the best year I've seen in the seven that I've been here," she said.

With rooms being booked up so early in the year, the KVA, City and Chamber of Commerce are forming preliminary strategies to deal with a seen with no rooms available.

One idea brought up at last week's council meeting is to build temporary wall tents in the clearing between Craven

Bluff and the Dome Road.

Van Nostrand said this is only one possible solution.

"There are some informal preliminary discussions about making contingency plans for overbooked days," he said.

For long-term tourism benefits, Van Nostrand said Dawson has to attract people during

the shoulder seasons to stretch the tourism season to four or five months. He said the construction of a bridge over the Yukon River is imperative.

"If we had a bridge built, we would have already had people here from Alaska and people going to Alaska."

The Gerties' Girls are just one of the many local attractions luring people to the Yukon.

The restart of the Dawson City Insider promoted a
positive business-friendly town.